Dear Cassandra,
Merry Christ[mas]
Much love
Peggy

Austin & Hill Country Celebrity Cookbook

Royalties Benefit the Austin Parks Foundation

Sheila Liermann & Nancy Reid

Austin & Hill Country Celebrity Cookbook

Copyright © 1996 by Sheila Liermann and Nancy Reid

All rights reserved. No part of this book may be reproduced in any form, except for brief reviews, without the written consent of the publisher.

Published by Lost Trail Productions, Inc.
Post Office Box 6160
Ketchum, Idaho 83340
208-788-5055 or 208-389-9169

Printed in Austin, Texas, United States of America

Book and cover design by Joan Donnelly, JD Graphics, Ketchum, Idaho
Cover art by Will Caldwell

ISBN: 0-9649428-1-X

Grateful acknowledgment is made to the following for permission to reprint previously published or copyrighted material:
   From *Along the Garden Path* by Bill and Sylvia Varney. Copyright © 1995 by Bill and Sylvia Varney. Fredericksburg Herb Farm. Reprinted by permission of the author.
   Ruby's El Paso 1949 Pasta by Texas Bix Bender, Copyright © 1996 by Texas Bix Bender. Printed by permission of the author.
   From *Don't Squat with Yer Spurs On: A Cowboy's Guide to Life* by Texas Bix Bender. © 1992 by Texas Bix Bender. Gibbs Smith, Publisher/Peregrine Smith Book Publishers. Reprinted by permission of the author.
   From *The Camera Never Blinks Twice: The Further Adventures of a Television Journalist* by Dan Rather. Copyright © 1994 by Dan Rather. William Morrow & Company, Incorporated. Reprinted by permission of the author.
   Anhydrous Zucchini by Steven Weinberg from *But the Crackling is Superb: An Anthology on Food and Drink by Fellow and Foreign Members of the Royal Society*, editors Nicholas Kurti and Giana Kurti. Copyright © 1988 IOP Publishing Ltd and individual contributors. Reprinted by permission of the author.

Lost Trail Productions, Inc. books are available at special discounts when purchased in bulk, as well as for fund-raising or educational use. For details, contact the Sales Director at the address above.

All royalties benefit the Austin Parks Foundation, Austin, Texas.

10 9 8 7 6 5 4 3 2

Table of Contents

Troy Aikman *A Cowboy's Favorite Meat Loaf* 6
Christine Albert *Lone Star Pasta Sauce* 7
Raúl Allegre *Kickin' Chicken Chipotle* 8
Bill Arhos *No Limits Chicken* 9
Susan and Ed Auler *Fall Creek Basil and Raspberry Shrimp Pasta* 10
Austin Angler *Larry's Almost Thai Chicken Soup* 11
Austin Lounge Lizards *Not-for-the-Capsicum-Impaired Salmon* 12
Austin Parks Foundation *Zilker Park Picnic for 50* 13
Bad Rodeo *After the Gig Migas* 14
Marcia Ball *Heart of Louisiana Etouffée* 15
Barbara Barrie *Mrs. Barney Miller's Chicken and Mushrooms* 16
Barton Creek Resort *Barton Creek Lobster and Vodka Gazpacho* 17
Lou Ann Barton *Passionate Lentil and Spinach Soup* 18
Paul Begala *Sunday Morning Banana Buttermilk Pancakes* 19
Texas Bix Bender *Ruby's El Paso 1949 Pasta* 20
Ray Benson *The Wheel's Corn Soup* 22
Bevo *Bevo Tackles Pork* 23
Sinclair Black *Chutney Lime Chicken* 24
Boerne Village Band *German Pioneer Whole Wheat Bread* 25
Doyle Bramhall *Good and Healthy Chicken Broth* 26
Broken Spoke *The Broken Spoke's Chicken Fried Steak with Cream Gravy* 27
William Broyles Jr. *Chicken Kale Soup* 28
Janelle Buchanan *Greenbelt Chicken and Brown Rice Salad* 29
Bob Bullock *Brown Beans by Bullock* 30
Barbara & George Bush *Fabulous Noodle Kugel* 31
George W. Bush *Statehouse Pecan Pie* 32
Laura Bush *Blueberry Sweet Potato Bread* 33
Earl Campbell *Earl Campbell's Sausage Jambalaya* 34
Sarah Elizabeth Campbell *Bummer Summer Salad* 35
Eugene Cernan *The Ultimate Chicken Spaghetti* 36
Fran Christina *Jane's Drunken Chicken 'n' Dumplins* 37
Chuy's *Chuy's Tex-Mex Chili Con Carne* 38
Jody Conradt *Slam Dunk Oatmeal Cookies* 39
Ben Crenshaw *A Master's Creamed Corn* 40
Roberta Crenshaw *Goodie Bars* 41
Elizabeth Crook *As Promised Texas Pralines* 42
Josh Davis *Fat-Freestyle Turkey Chili* 43
Libby Doggett *Lloyd's Favorite Gingerbread* 44
Robert Draper *Circle J Pumpkin Risotto* 45
The Driskill *Marinated Portobello Mushrooms with Black Bean Sauce* 46
Chris Duarte *Shade Tree Banana Pudding* 47
Ruth Ellsworth & Bill Carter *Inside the Eastside Tomato Basil Soup* 48
Joe Ely *Gypsy Cowboy Posole* 49
Michael Fracasso *Insalata Pasta e Fagioli* 50
Fredericksburg Brewing Company *Jamaican Jerked Emu with Mango Chutney* 51
Fredericksburg Herb Farm *Rosemary and Orange Rum Cake with Glorious Glaze* 52
Kinky Friedman *The Kinkster's Chicken Piccata* 53
Steven Fromholz *Go Native Marinade* 54
Héctor Galán *Director Héctor Salsa* 55
Jimmie Dale Gilmore *Janet's Spinach Enchiladas* 56
Laura Groppe *A Girl's German Potato Salad* 57
Kelly Gruber *La Zona Rosa's Pasta Gruber* 58
Cliff Gustafson *Coach Gus' Swedish Pancakes* 59
David Halley *Poetic Potato Leek Soup* 60
Thomas "Hollywood" Henderson *Hollywood's Chili Beans* 61
Hill Country Fruit Council *Grandma's Chilled Peach Pie* 62
Tish Hinojosa *Traditional Ancho Sauce* 63
Champ Hood *River City Green Bean Rolls* 64
Tobe Hooper *Texas Chainsaw Chili* 65
Kay Bailey Hutchison *Shadywood Showdown Chili* 66
The Instruments *Brownies for Lazy, Decadent People* 68
Molly Ivins *Hungarian Paprika Mushrooms* 69
Johnny Dee and the Rocket 88s *White Scratch Cake with Texas Pecan Icing* 70
Eric Johnson *Roasted Red Bell Pepper Pesto* 71
Lady Bird Johnson *LBJ Ranch Spicy Cheddar Wafers* 72
Milton Jung *Arresting Barbecued Pork Loin Chops* 73

Emily Kaitz *Dreaded Yuppie Sun-dried Tomato Pesto* 74
Beverly Kearney *Make Tracks Chicken* 75
Robert Earl Keen *Sonora Death Row Casserole* 76
Jimmy LaFave *Rave LaFave Veggie Chili* 77
Lake Austin Spa Resort *Sweet Potato Crab Cakes and Rémoulade* 78
Lake Travis Bed and Breakfast *Sail Away Breakfast Soufflé* 79
Dana Lewis *Pattypan Squash with a Twist* 80
David L. Lindsey *Lonesome Dove and Wild Rice* 81
Richard Linklater *Epicurean Slacker's Delight* 82
Jerry Long *A Roper's Breakfast* 83
James Lovell *Out-of-this-World Crab Strata* 84
John Mackovic *Mac Attack Pasta* 85
Iain Matthews *Veronique's Apple Pie* 86
Ed Mayberry *Mayberry Applesauce Cake* 87
Delbert McClinton *Sauced on Tequila Shrimp* 88
Red McCombs *Go to Hell Prime Rib* 89
James Michener *James Michener's Beef Bourguignon* 90
Ed Miller *A Scot's Dutch Witloof by Way of Texas* 91
Abra Moore *More Mango Pie, Please* 92
Azie Taylor Morton *A Treasure of a Tamale Pie* 93
Michael Martin Murphey *Grandma's Ham Hallelujah* 94
Cecilia Nasti *A Woman on the Verge of Herbed Orzo* 95
Gary P. Nunn *Züricher Geschnitzeltes* 96
Joe Nick Patoski *My Ladies' Greek Chicken* 97
Tom Penders *Coach Penders' Breakfast Tacos* 98
Jo Carol Pierce *Twice-Naked Pesto* 99
Toni Price *Barn Dance Potluck Potato Salad* 100
Jenna Beth Radtke *New Mexico Corn Bake* 101
Tomás Ramirez *Migas al Chino* 102
John Randall *The Most Famous Hot Sauce In Texas* 103
Dan Rather *My Mom's Vinegar Pie* 104
Jan Reid *Rosemary Garlic Roasted Potatoes* 105
George Reiff *Lyle Loved It Tart* 106
Mary Lou Retton *Paella to Flip Over* 107
Ann Richards *Firecracker Cornbread* 108
Charlie Robison *Honey Butter and Jalapeño Dove* 109
Johnny Rodriguez *Fresh Rodriguez Pico de Gallo* 110
Robert Rodriguez *Desperate for Pecan Pie* 111

Darrell Royal *Dewberry Cobbler* 112
Ruby's BBQ *Kate's Grilled Rack of Lamb* 113
Ben Sargent *Pollo y Arroz Texas Style* 114
Joe Sears *Pearl's Molasses Snaps* 115
Beverly Sheffield *Beat the Heat Eat Dessert* 116
Jane Sibley *Tequila Lemon Pie* 117
Sincola *Sinful Texas Tacos* 118
Julie Speed *Speedy Pasta e Fagioli* 119
Jill Sterkel *Roadhouse Pizza* 120
Jim Talbot *Pasta Talbot* 121
Travis County Farmers' Market *Award Winning Texas Sweet Peach Cobbler* 122
John Travolta *Phenomenal Grilled Polenta and Wild Mushroom Napoleon* 123
Rick Trevino *Doctor Time's Cheese Enchiladas* 125
Charles Trois *Très Trois Tuna Spaghetti* 126
Tommy Tune *Papa Tune's Red Eye Gravy* 127
Merlin Tuttle *Congress Avenue Spicy Shrimp* 128
Jimmie Vaughan *Family Style Hot Spaghetti* 129
Barry Waite *Motorolan Moussaka* 130
Jerry Jeff Walker *King Ranch Chicken* 131
Don Walser *Jailhouse Rolls* 133
Monte Warden *Mima's Chicken Fried Steak* 134
Sarah Weddington *Fort Smith Apple Pie* 135
Steven Weinberg *Anhydrous Zucchini* 136
Shannon Wheeler *Shannon Wheeler's Bachelor Burritos* 137
Wiley Wiggins *Dazed and Confused Lasagna* 138
Van Wilks *Wok 'n' Roll Yardbird Stir Fry* 139
Jaston Williams *Vera's Lime Pie* 140
Lucinda Williams *Secret of Longevity Sweet Corn Bread* 141
Kim Wilson *Italian Cream Cake* 142
Marion Winik *My Father's Tuna Spread* 143
Bill Wittliff *Mexican Cabrito Frito* 144
Sandy Wood *Stellar Dessert Meringues* 145
Charles Alan Wright *Microwave Chocolate Bread Pudding* 146
Y.O. Ranch *Bertie's Y.O. Venison* 147
Ziller House *Dill Crusted Salmon with Corn and Asparagus Relish* 148
Nadya Zybine and Rafael Padilla *Havana Pork Chops* 149

AUSTIN PARKS FOUNDATION

When you ask residents to describe what they like best about Austin, odds are that the city's magnificent parks, trails, public swimming holes, and preserves will be at or near the top of the list. Austin's green spaces are at the heart of its identity, and Austinites are passionate about preserving and improving them.

People gather at Zilker Park and Austin's many neighborhood parks with their families and friends for celebrations, picnics and reunions. Austin parks provide the perfect settings for potato salad, laughter, and the kind of times that keep us together as family, friends, and communities.

Austin residents associate certain parks with momentous moments. They are the places where first kisses are planted, where toddlers gleefully swing, and where winning homers are hit while grateful teammates cheer. Memories are made in parks.

And for many, our parks are places for introspection. In the open space and under the rustling leaves, we have found moments to escape everyday concerns and to reflect; to contemplate our place on earth. Parks are every man's and every woman's Walden Pond, Bodh Gaya tree, and reachable sanctuary.

The Austin Parks Foundation was founded in 1992 to assure that there would be plenty of green open spaces for the city's growing population. We are a grassroots, mostly volunteer, charitable organization dedicated to supporting Austin parks by providing critically needed services and funding in partnership with public and private organizations. Some of our accomplishments are: funding of the Springdale Park, and redevelopment of Bartholomew Park and the Allison Elementary School Playground; establishment of the Junior Lifeguard Scholarship Program for low-income students; and a commitment to help build the 364-acre Colorado River Park.

With continuing cuts in the city's Parks and Recreation budget, the Board of Directors of the Austin Parks Foundation believes that its work is just beginning.

The *Austin and Hill Country Celebrity Cookbook* contributors—musicians, artists, actors, scientists, athletes, cartoonists, directors, business leaders and a host of others—also believe that people need open, natural spaces within its civilizations to remain civilized. We'd like to thank all our contributors for generously donating their time and for sending us a recipe. Their contribution, and your contribution (we receive a royalty from each cookbook sold), will go toward reaching our goals and helping Austin remain one of the last great places to live.

We hope you enjoy our cookbook and the stories behind the recipes. It's a great reflection of what Austin has to offer—friendly folks. We also hope you enjoy the wonderful recipes passed on to us. You'll find family culinary treasures, imaginative concoctions, and easy, no-fuss fare, perfect for a picnic in a park!

Have you been to the park, lately?

Paula Fracasso, Executive Director
The Austin Parks Foundation

Troy Aikman

A Cowboy's Favorite Meat Loaf

This is Troy's favorite home-cooked meal at his Mom's house. You can adjust the bread crumbs and barbecue sauce ratio, depending upon your preference for moistness and spiciness.

2	pounds ground beef
1	cup seasoned bread crumbs or stuffing mix
1	egg, beaten
½	cup milk
½	cup barbecue sauce
2	tablespoons chopped green pepper
1	small onion, chopped
1	tablespoon fresh basil, thinly sliced
½	cup grated Cheddar cheese, or more to taste
½	cup grated Monterey Jack cheese, or more to taste
	salt and pepper to taste

When Troy Aikman was selected as one of *People* magazine's most beautiful people, he said with his usual self-deprecating humor, "Well, they must not know very many people." The shy, soft-spoken Dallas Cowboy quarterback has never taken much to the limelight that goes with being a "national football hero." Troy was called one of the "best quarterbacks in the NFL" by no less an authority than Roger Staubach himself. Among his many honors, Troy was named Super Bowl XXVII's Most Valuable Player. The son of a pipeline construction worker/rancher and a homemaker, Troy likes to relax by listening to live country music in Austin, working on his computer, and socializing with longtime friends and family members. He is the founder of the Troy Aikman Foundation, which benefits children's charities.

Preheat oven to 350°.

Place the ground beef in a large mixing bowl. In a separate mixing bowl, combine the bread crumbs or stuffing mix with the egg, milk, and barbecue sauce.

Add the bread crumb mixture to the beef, and mix well. Stir in green pepper, onion, and basil.

Spread the meat loaf mixture on a square of tin foil. Meat mixture should be ½ inch thick on the foil. Layer the cheeses over meat to within one inch of the edges. Roll up the tin foil jelly-roll fashion, and pinch foil all around to seal.

Place the meat loaf in a 9x5x3-inch loaf pan, seam-side down. Bake for 1 hour.

Remove from the tin foil, and serve on a platter. Serves 6–8

Christine Albert

Lone Star Pasta Sauce

Christine notes that non-Texans can use another sausage if Meyers is not available, but Meyers sausages are best.

- 2 tablespoon butter
- 1 medium onion, diced
- 3 cloves garlic, minced
- 1 pound ground turkey or ground beef
- ½ pound mushrooms, cleaned and sliced
- ½ pound Meyers sausage, sliced into ½-inch rounds
- 1 green pepper, diced (optional)
- 2 15-ounce cans tomato sauce
- 1 6-ounce can tomato paste
- 3 tablespoons red wine
- 1 teaspoon dried oregano
- 1 bay leaf
- 1 pound pasta, cooked according to instructions

In a large stock pot, melt the butter over medium heat. Add the onion and garlic and cook until limp, about 5 minutes. Add the ground meat, mushrooms, sausage, pepper, and cook until meat is no longer pink. Stir in the tomato sauce, tomato paste, red wine, oregano, and bay leaf, and simmer 2–3 hours. You may need to add water if the sauce gets too thick.

Serve over your choice of pasta noodles. Serves 4–6

Some things are distinctly Texan. The Alamo. Bluebonnets. The Dallas Cowboys. Shiner Bock Beer. And Christine Albert. Her most recent album, *Underneath the Lone Star Sky*, is pure Texas country-rock. The album, her third, focuses on her love of high energy and intelligent modern-country music. Since 1982, the New York native has been a mainstay of the Texas music scene, and says living in Austin has, "pushed me to keep growing…. My music has evolved out of the sounds of this community." And although the power of Nashville pulls at Christine, she chooses to stay in Austin. "…I have always needed to get on stage and play my songs for an audience. Austin is such a great live music center."

Raúl Allegre

Raúl Allegre must be extremely *allegre* about his life accomplishments to date. Born and raised in the agricultural city of Torreón in northern Mexico, Raúl began his football career as an exchange student in Shelton, Washington. With the precision of a Rolex, he developed a world-class kicking style. As a pro, Raúl became one of the most successful field goal kickers ever for both the Baltimore Colts and the New York Jets. The former NFL All-Pro Kicker played in two New York Giants' Super Bowls, winning both times. After retiring from the NFL, Raúl returned to Austin, the home of his alma mater, the University of Texas. Presently, he is president of Laguna Entertainment & Marketing. Through his company and numerous community projects, Raúl has projected a positive image for many Latino teens.

Kickin' Chicken Chipotle

Raúl is right on target with this recipe. The chicken absorbs the flavors of the chipotle and bacon, and the sumptuous cream sauce balances the heat from the peppers.

- 6 boneless, chicken breasts, skinned
- 6 strips bacon
- 2 cups (1 pint) heavy cream
- 2 chipotle peppers (canned or fresh), seeded and chopped
- 2 tablespoons butter
- 1 teaspoon cornstarch
  salt to taste

Preheat oven to 350°.

Wrap each chicken breast with a strip of bacon, and sauté in butter for one minute per side. Set in a glass, ovenproof pan, and cook in oven for 20 minutes. Remove chicken from pan and drain off excess grease. Replace chicken in baking pan.

In a small mixing bowl, combine cream, chipotle peppers, cornstarch, and salt. Pour mixture over chicken breasts and return to oven for another 10–20 minutes or until the sauce has thickened and breasts are cooked through.

Serve with rice. Serves 6

Bill Arhos

No Limits Chicken

Please note that the chicken needs to marinate overnight. After your first tangy bite, you'll find that planning ahead is well worth the effort.

1	3-pound chicken, cut into serving pieces
1	tablespoon salt
1	teaspoon oregano
2	lemons
4–6	medium potatoes, peeled and cut into quarters (or 10–12 small red potatoes, halved)
4	tablespoons olive oil, divided
	salt and pepper to taste
½	cup water

Wash the chicken and pat dry. Put the pieces in a non-reactive bowl, and sprinkle with oregano and salt. Juice 1 lemon and drizzle the juice over the chicken. Cover and refrigerate overnight.

Preheat oven to 350°.

Place the potatoes in a bowl, and add 2 tablespoons of the olive oil. Toss the potatoes to coat. Sprinkle with salt and pepper. (The chicken is also salted, so use salt sparingly.) Arrange the potatoes in a large casserole. Remove the chicken from the refrigerator. Pour 2 tablespoons olive oil over the chicken, coating each piece. Arrange the chicken over the potatoes. Squeeze the juice from the remaining lemon, and pour over the chicken and potatoes. Bake, covered, for 1 hour. Remove the cover, and add ½ cup water. Cook the chicken, uncovered, until golden-brown, about 30 more minutes. Serves 4

In 1976, most country-music careers were launched from what was then the epicenter of country—Nashville. But Bill Arhos saw the burgeoning music scene in Austin and decided to take advantage of it when he showcased an obscure local musician—the now wildly famous Willie Nelson, for the *Austin City Limits* television pilot. The rest is history, both for Willie and *Austin City Limits*, what is now the longest-running show on PBS and the most popular music series on television. In its third decade, the show reflects Bill's love for all types of music and often strays beyond the country genre into blues, rock, Tejano, folk, and jazz. When the former semi-pro baseball player isn't creating new shows at the KLRU television studios or working on his antique knife collection, he can be found casting a line in one of the Austin area's great fishing spots.

Winemaking in Texas is a long-standing art, dating back to the 1600s when Spanish missionaries brought grapevine cuttings to the Lone Star state to produce sacramental wine. However, Texas wines didn't gain national fame for another 370 years. Ed and Susan Auler, owners of Fall Creek Vineyards, are partly responsible for that long overdue recognition. They started a 65-acre vineyard on the shores of Lake Buchanan in 1975, and today produce award-winning wines. Ed, the vintor, takes advantage of the superb Hill Country climate and traditional European techniques. Susan, a former interior decorator, serves as the company's director of marketing. Austinites look forward every August to the annual Fall Creek Vineyards' Grape Stomp, and the opportunity to taste the latest bottle from the winery.

Susan & Ed Auler

Fall Creek Basil and Raspberry Shrimp Pasta

Susan Auler suggests serving this delightful pasta with a 1988 Fall Creek Vineyards Semillon-Sauvignon Blanc.

Shrimp:
- 2 tablespoons butter
- ⅓ cup minced green onion
- 4 garlic cloves, minced
- 1 pound shrimp, peeled and deveined
- 1 tablespoon raspberry vinegar
- 2 tablespoons minced fresh basil
- salt and pepper to taste

Sauce:
- ½ cup butter
- 8 ounces heavy cream
- ¾ cup grated fresh Parmesan cheese

- 10 ounces fettuccini

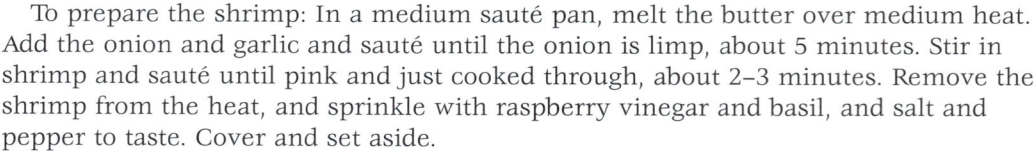

To prepare the shrimp: In a medium sauté pan, melt the butter over medium heat. Add the onion and garlic and sauté until the onion is limp, about 5 minutes. Stir in shrimp and sauté until pink and just cooked through, about 2–3 minutes. Remove the shrimp from the heat, and sprinkle with raspberry vinegar and basil, and salt and pepper to taste. Cover and set aside.

To prepare the sauce: In a sauce pan, melt the butter over low heat. Raise the heat to medium and add the cream and Parmesan cheese, and cook until the sauce is a smooth creamy texture.

Meanwhile, bring a large pot of water to a boil for the fettuccini. Cook fettuccini until al dente, about 6–8 minutes. Drain.

In a large, warmed pasta bowl, toss the fettuccini and sauce. Top with the shrimp and serve immediately. Serves 4

Austin Angler

Larry's Almost Thai Chicken Soup

For the best results, fresh ingredients are a must. But finding fresh lime leaves and lemon grass can be challenging. I now have a kaffir lime tree and lemon grass in pots on my deck. —Larry Sunderland

1	2½-pound whole chicken
2	quarts water
1	teaspoon salt
2	tablespoons red Thai chili pepper sauce
2	tablespoons Thai fish sauce
2	Thai pickled red peppers
10–12	slices fresh ginger
3–4	stalks fresh lemon grass, cut into 2-inch lengths and sliced lengthwise
2–3	kaffir lime leaves
8–10	straw mushrooms (optional)
10	cherry tomatoes, halved, or 2 Roma tomatoes, sliced

juice of 3 limes
1 bunch cilantro, rinsed and stems removed

Rinse chicken well and trim off all excess fat. Cut the chicken into quarters and place in a large soup pot. Add the water and salt, and bring to boil. Skim off the foam as it collects on the surface.

Cover, reduce the heat, and simmer for 1 hour. Remove the chicken from the stock. Let cool and remove meat from the bone. (If you have time, place the stock in refrigerator to harden the fat so that it can be easily removed.)

Pour stock through strainer into large soup pot. Add chili sauce, fish sauce, red peppers, ginger, lemon grass, and lime leaves, and mushrooms, if desired. Simmer for 30–45 minutes.

Return chicken meat to stock. Add tomatoes and simmer for 3–5 minutes. Ladle into individual soup bowls and squeeze 1 teaspoon lime juice into each bowl. Garnish with cilantro leaves and serve immediately. Serves 6–8

Austin Angler co-owners Larry Sunderland, Jim Adams, and Mina Hemingway are pioneers in the great Austin downtown revitalization. "For fifteen years we have patiently been sitting here waiting for everyone else to get it," Larry says. Located in the heart of Austin on Congress Street, the spot isn't the most logical for a fly-fishing store. But after 15 years, fly-fishing fanatics from all over the state—and even the nation—seek out the Austin Angler for the best selection of flies, poles, reels, and other equipment. The Austin Angler is now the oldest specialty fly-fishing shop in Texas. For Larry, success is sweet, as long as he still has time for fishing.

Austin Lounge Lizards

Steve Clark

Original satirical bluegrass has been the trademark of the Austin Lounge Lizards since 1980. With hits like *Jesus Loves Me (But He Can't Stand You)*, *Gingrich The Newt*, and *Shallow End of the Gene Pool*, the Lizards are a favorite hometown band, and have been honored several times in the *Austin Chronicle* Readers' Poll. They have also toured nationwide (38 states, so far) and have been featured on National Public Radio's *Morning Edition* and TNN. Lizard CDs include *Creatures From the Black Saloon*, *Highway Cafe of the Damned*, *Lizard Vision*, and *Paint Me on Velvet*. The band's lineup includes Conrad Deisler, Tom Pittman, Hank Card (who still manages to practice as a part-time administrative law judge for the State of Texas), Richard Bowden, and Boo Resnick.

Not-for-the-Capsicum-Impaired Salmon

This is an easy way to prepare a piece of fresh salmon. I adapted it from a recipe developed by my mom. We usually serve this with a steamed vegetable, like asparagus or broccoli, and lemon risotto or grilled polenta. —Conrad Deisler, band guitarist

1	24-ounce fillet of the freshest salmon you can find, cut from the thickest portion of the fish

Marinade:
1½	cups soy sauce
4	cloves garlic, crushed or minced
1	tablespoon red pepper sauce (for the capsicum-impaired, substitute 1 tablespoon lemon juice)
1–2	tablespoons olive oil

Combine marinade ingredients, mixing thoroughly.

Rinse and dry fillet and place it fleshy side down in marinade in large glass pan. Allow fish to marinate for about 1 hour at room temperature or all day in the refrigerator.

Preheat oven to 500°.

Pat salmon dry and rub olive oil on top and sides of fillet. Place salmon, skin side down, on an oiled broiler pan.

Turn oven to broil and broil fish, with oven door shut, for about 5 minutes. The salmon should be about 3 inches from the broiler. Turn oven off and leave salmon in the hot oven for about 10 more minutes. The salmon should be opaque and flaky, but still moist. Serves 4

Austin Parks Foundation

Zilker Park Picnic for 50

A wonderful recipe for an Italian potato salad. It's perfect for a picnic in one of Austin's great parks.

10	pounds small new potatoes
1	bunch rosemary
2½	cups extra virgin olive oil
1	whole celery head
	lots of salt

    Scrub but don't peel potatoes. Bring a very large pot of water to boil with the rosemary and some salt. Boil the potatoes until tender, about 15–20 minutes.
    Drain potatoes and let them cool. Discard the rosemary.
    Clean and finely chop the celery, leaves and all.
    Put all the ingredients in a large bowl with lots of salt and mix well. Serve at room temperature. Serves your 50 closest friends

The Austin Parks Foundation is a grassroots, charitable foundation created in 1992 to protect one of Austin's crucial resources—its open spaces. In these days of dwindling public funds and increasing demand for parks, the Foundation works closely with the City of Austin Parks and Recreation Department to address many needs—from park development to youth leadership programs. The Foundation receives grants and donations, develops projects without the cost of city overhead, and involves hundreds of volunteers. The Foundation is the brainchild of Beverly Griffith, who served as its president through its early years, and now is a member of the Austin City Council. The current president is David Adair. Paula Fracasso is the Foundation's executive director.

Bad Rodeo

After the Gig Migas

Bad Rodeo's manager, George Barton, submits this recipe on behalf of the band. Migas are great after a night out on the town or after a lazy sleep-in-kind-of-morning.

1	tablespoon oil or butter
1	medium onion, chopped
10	corn tortillas
12	eggs, lightly beaten
1	jalapeño, finely chopped
	salt and pepper to taste
	picante sauce to taste
1	cup grated Monterey Jack cheese

Contrary to popular Western myth, there is such a thing as a bad rodeo in Texas. Bad Rodeo is a down-and-dirty *band* comprised of Dan Tucker and Jeff Reynolds. The two made their debut in March of 1991 at the Austin/Travis County Livestock Show and Rodeo BBQ Cookoff. Since their first appearance, public demand for Bad Rodeo's country-rock-blues style of music has been remarkable. They perform a grueling weekly schedule for eager fans, and have two recordings, *Texas Country Rockin' Blues* and the self-titled *Bad Rodeo*, in music stores.

In a large skillet, heat the oil or butter over medium heat. Add onion and sauté until soft, about 5 minutes. While the onion is cooking, cut the corn tortillas into pieces, about one-inch square. Add the tortillas to the onion (adding more oil, if necessary), and stir to coat the tortillas lightly with oil. Heat through.

Meanwhile, in a mixing bowl, beat together the eggs, jalapeño, salt and pepper, and picante sauce. Add the egg mixture to the skillet, and stir occasionally until the eggs are just firm. Sprinkle the cheese on top of the eggs, and cover until cheese is melted, about 1 minute. Top with additional picante sauce, if desired, and serve. Serves 6–8

Marcia Ball

Heart of Louisiana Etouffée

Etouffée captures the essence of seafood. Keep it simple. —Marcia Ball

- 2 large onions, finely chopped
- 1 cup celery, finely chopped
- 1 bell pepper, chopped
- 3 garlic cloves, minced
- ½ cup olive oil
- ½ cup (1 stick) butter
- 3 pounds medium shrimp or crawfish tails, peeled and deveined
- 3 teaspoons paprika
- pinch of cayenne pepper
- salt and pepper to taste
- 1 heaping tablespoon all-purpose flour
- 1 cup parsley, chopped and divided
- 1 bunch green onion tops, chopped

In a 4-quart saucepan, sauté onion, celery, bell pepper, and garlic in the oil and butter over low-medium heat until the vegetables have wilted, about 5 minutes. Stir in the shrimp, paprika, cayenne, and salt and pepper.

Cover and cook over low heat for 7 minutes, stirring several times. Then stir in flour and half the parsley. Cover and simmer for 5 more minutes, or until shrimp turn a solid pink color.

Taste and adjust seasonings.

Serve over white rice, garnishing with onion tops and remaining parsley. Put Tabasco and Louisiana hot sauce on the table for those who like it hot. *Bon appétit!* Serves 6

Marcia Ball was born into a big, old Louisiana family in Vinton, a small town in what she calls "the heart of a great fertile musical ground." She is a fourth-generation musician, who took up the piano because there were pianos in her house—and in those of her relatives and neighbors. Marcia moved to Austin in 1970, and is married to former La Zona Rosa owner Gordon Fowler, an artist. On stage, the six-foot boogie-woogie queen is unforgettable. She's been described as a triple threat: one of the best blues singers in the country, a New Orleans-style piano pyrotechnician, and a fantastic live performer. And one more thing, don't overlook her formidable songwriting, as witnessed in her latest release *Blue House*.

Barbara Barrie

The stage and the page have been Barbara Barrie's claim to fame. Born and raised in Corpus Christi, Barbara struck out in her teens for Austin and the University of Texas. But the theater called her and she moved to New York City, where Barbara has made an impressive career. She's had major roles in such Broadway plays as *Prisoner of Second Avenue*, *California Suite*, and *Company*, for which she received a Tony nomination. And Barbara also made her mark in Hollywood in *One Potato, Two Potato*, *Private Benjamin*, and *Breaking Away*, for which she received an Academy Award nomination. She was Elisabeth Miller on television's *Barney Miller*. She is the author of two books for young adults—*Lone Star* and *Adam Zigzag*.

Mrs. Barney Miller's Chicken and Mushrooms

Barbara's friend, Mary Eckhardt White, gave her this elegant recipe for a dish that's great for company or a special family dinner. Barbara and Mary have been friends since attending the same fourth-grade class in Corpus Christi.

- 5 chicken breasts, skinned
- 1½ cups chicken stock, preferably homemade
- ½ medium red onion, chopped
- 2 tablespoons olive oil
- 3 cloves garlic, minced
- 1 fresh jalapeño pepper, finely chopped
- 1 large shallot, chopped
- 1 tablespoon chili powder
- ½ teaspoon chili oil
- 1 teaspoon dry oregano, or to taste
- 1 teaspoon dry basil, or to taste
- ¼ teaspoon salt
- 1 tablespoon all-purpose flour
- 1 28-ounce can crushed tomatoes, drained
- 2 tablespoons Madeira wine, or sherry
- ¼ cup vermouth
- 1 tablespoon maple syrup
- 1 teaspoon Champagne vinegar, or to taste
- ½ pound (2½–3 cups) mushrooms, sliced

Poach chicken breasts in chicken stock for 8–10 minutes over medium-high heat. Breasts should be opaque and juices should run clear when meat is pierced. Remove from heat and uncover, allowing to cool in broth. When the broth is lukewarm, remove breasts to a plate. Clean bones from breasts and cut meat into finger-sized slices. Set aside. Skim off excess fat from broth and cook down remaining broth to 1 cup.

In a large sauté pan over medium-low heat, cook onion in half the oil until soft, 5–10 minutes, adding garlic, jalapeño, and shallot after a few minutes. Stir in chili powder, chili oil, oregano, basil, and salt. Turn heat to medium and add flour, stirring continuously, until mixture bubbles and cooks slightly, about 1 minute. Then add concentrated chicken broth, and stir over medium heat until thickened. Add crushed tomatoes.

Lower heat so that sauce simmers and add Madeira, vermouth, maple syrup, and Champagne vinegar. Simmer for 10–15 minutes. Taste and adjust seasoning.

Meanwhile, sauté mushrooms in the remaining oil over medium in a large sauté pan for 5–10 minutes or until tender.

Add chicken and mushrooms to sauce. Heat through. Serve hot over rice or pasta. Serves 6

Barton Creek Resort

Barton Creek Lobster and Vodka Gazpacho

This recipe was created by executive chef Philip R. Bouza. Chef Bouza's specialties include gourmet cuisine and unique sauces influenced by his years at the Culinary Institute of America in Hyde Park, New York.

- 3 lobster tails, shells split and cleaned
- 3 8-ounce cans V-8 Juice
- 2 8-ounce cans Red Eye Bloody Mary mix
- 1 ounce vodka
- 1 English-style cucumber, finely diced
- 1 small red onion, finely diced
- 3 celery stalks, thinly sliced on the diagonal
- 2 japaleño peppers, seeded and diced
- 2 red tomatoes, seeded and diced
- 2 yellow tomatoes, seeded and diced
- juice from 1 fresh lime
- 1 bunch fresh cilantro, stems removed and leaves chopped, reserving 8 springs for garnish
- salt and pepper to taste

In a large pot, steam the lobster meat for 5–7 minutes. Set aside to cool. Meanwhile, combine the V-8 juice, Bloody Mary mix, and vodka in a large stainless steel bowl. Add the cucumber, red onion, celery, jalapeño, and tomatoes. Mix well. Stir in the fresh lime juice and chopped fresh cilantro.

Remove the lobster meat from the shells, and slice thin. Discard shells. Add the lobster meat to the soup mixture, and refrigerate overnight. Serve in a chilled bowl, and garnish with the fresh cilantro sprigs. Serves 8

Sprawling out over 4,000 acres of woods and rolling hills in West Austin, Barton Creek Resort is a golfer's mecca with three spectacular courses designed by golf greats Tom Fazio, Ben Crenshaw, Bill Coore, and Arnold Palmer. If you don't swing a club, you can swing a racket on one of the resort's twelve outdoor tennis courts or jog along a track with breathtaking views of the Hill Country. A European-style spa includes a state-of-the-art health and fitness facility and massage services for when your muscles can take no more. Dining at the resort can be relaxed or of the black-tie variety.

Lou Ann Barton

Mark Guerra

Lou Ann Barton has been called "The most commanding white female belter to erupt out of Texas since Janis Joplin…." "A buzz saw fueled by honey…." "Honest and unapologetically passionate, Barton is that most appealing of nature's forces: a natural woman." "Barton's voice…is an instrument powerful enough to strip the chrome from cars in the parking lot." Or as Linda Ronstadt observes, "This woman scares me to death."

These are just some of the words used to describe the Texas spitfire, "Miss Lou Ann." A Fort Worth girl whose daddy drove a truck and whose mama runs a bookstore, Lou Ann has been in the national limelight for more than a decade. In 1982, *Old Enough* was the only debut album of the year to appear on MTV's Top Ten list, and it received a "four star" rating from *Rolling Stone*. *Read My Lips* continues that legacy. At home in Austin, Lou Ann is loved fanatically.

Passionate Lentil and Spinach Soup

A wonderful recipe for soup that is healthy, lowfat, and at the same time appealing and satisfying.

1	cup dry lentils
1	cup chopped celery
5	cups chicken stock
2	garlic cloves, minced
1/8	teaspoon cayenne pepper
1	medium onion, chopped
1	cup sliced carrot
1/2	teaspoon grated lemon peel
1	cup cooked ham, chopped (optional)
1	pound fresh spinach, rinsed, drained and chopped

Rinse and drain lentils in a soup pot. Add all ingredients except ham and spinach. Bring to a boil and simmer, covered, for 45 minutes. Add ham and simmer 15 minutes more, uncovered. Stir in fresh spinach and cook until just wilted. Serve immediately. Serves 4

Paul Begala

Sunday Morning Banana Buttermilk Pancakes

After nine months on the road during the 1992 presidential campaign, Paul came home jubilant, exhausted, and about 20 pounds overweight. He immediately started a new regimen of daily exercise and a low-fat diet. Now he runs about 90 miles a month, and sticks closely to a healthy diet that includes recipes like the one I've submitted. He weighs less and looks better than he did ten years ago! —Diane Begala

- 1 cup flour
- 2 tablespoons cornmeal
- 1 tablespoon sugar
- 1 teaspoon baking powder
- ½ teaspoon baking soda
- ½ teaspoon salt
- ⅛ teaspoon cinnamon
- 1⅓ cups buttermilk
- 1 egg or ¼ cup egg substitute
- 1 large ripe banana, mashed

In a large mixing bowl, combine the flour, cornmeal, sugar, baking powder, baking soda, salt, and cinnamon. Mix well.

In a smaller bowl, whisk together the buttermilk and egg. Stir the wet ingredients into the dry ingredients, but do not over mix. Fold in the banana.

Heat a griddle over medium-high, and spray with non-stick cooking spray. Ladle batter onto griddle, using about ¼ cup of batter per pancake. Cook pancakes until undersides are golden and bubbles are popping on the surface. Flip, and cook for 1–2 more minutes. Repeat. Serves 2–3

Before the author of *Primary Colors* was discovered, Paul Begala was listed among those who were close enough to the Clinton campaign to have written it. Paul and partner James Carville helped install Clinton in the White House in 1992, and Paul was Clinton's favorite phrasemaker. He coined the witticism, "It's the economy, stupid." Paul left the Beltway in 1995 for Austin to teach a course on politics and the press at his alma mater, the University of Texas, to run a public relations firm, to write a column for John F. Kennedy Jr.'s magazine, *George*, and, as he says, to get a life. Paul and his wife, Diane, have two children.

Texas Bix Bender

Ruby's El Paso 1949 Pasta

I'm not exactly sure of some of the details I am about to reveal about how I got this recipe. It was a long time ago, and a lot has happened since then.

Down in pretty far West Texas, along the border, not far from Esperanza, there was a little roadhouse run by an Italian by the name of Federico. He had come to America to be a tango dancer in New York. That dream ended and another one began when he fell in love with a trick ridin' cowgirl from San Angelo who had come to New York to ride in a rodeo at Madison Square Garden. They met at a dancing parlor where he was working. She and some rodeo pals had gone there to tango one evening after their rodeo show. Her name was Ruby. In the old photograph I saw of her, it was plain to see why what happened, happened. She fit her jeans in a pleasing well-packed manner. Her hair under her Stetson was long, blond, and curly. Her smile was a little crooked, yet enticing. Her face was smooth and seductive. Her eyes promised. She was dynamite looking for a light. And, from what he told me, Federico fell all over himself offering her one. She led him on a wild, wonderful, and very merry chase from New York to Chicago to Los Angeles to Dallas and on to El Paso. She wouldn't say yes, but she wouldn't say no. Maybe she thought it was sophisticated to have an Italian lover chasing her all over America. Whatever she thought, he thought it was heaven. It was in El Paso that he went to a tattoo parlor and had a heart with "Ruby, El Paso 1949" tattooed on his left bicep. When I asked him why El Paso, instead of any of the other cities they'd been in, he smiled. Big smile. Satisfied smile. We were sitting in his kitchen drinking a beer at the time. Through the open kitchen doors we could hear the jukebox playing out in the bar. The song was Ernest Tubb's **Waltz Across Texas**. Still smiling, he asked me if I was mangé? Italian for hungry. I was. "I fix for you," he said, "my most famous dish. The dish I fixed for Ruby, the night I got my tattoo."

Texas Bix Bender isn't a psychologist, but he has given sage advise to millions of people, and a few cowboys. His best-selling book *Don't Squat With Yer Spurs On—A Cowboy's Guide to Life* puts forth such rational counsel as: "Speak your mind, but ride a fast horse." Or, "Never lie unless you have to, and if you don't have a damn good lie, stick to the truth." Texas Bix spent his youth in the Hill Country, but he does not currently live in Texas. If he did, no one would call him Texas. He says you have to leave someplace to have it become your nickname. He has lived and worked everywhere from Austin to Antioch, including Hollywood. He quips, "I don't live in Hollywood anymore, either, but I would never allow anyone to call me Hollywood Bix Bender." He currently lives in Nashville, where he has a small chile ranch on the outskirts of town.

1	pound vermicelli or extra-thin spaghetti
¼	cup olive oil (In other words, enough to nicely cover the bottom of the skillet you're gonna use.)
1	tablespoon Worcestershire sauce
3	dashes Tabasco sauce
	black pepper to taste
½	head cabbage, chopped in slivers, or sliced into julienne, as some people say

2	carrots, chopped in slivers
2–3	garlic cloves, minced
1	small Texas sweet onion, chopped in slivers
	(No, there were no Texas sweets back then, but knowing Federico like I do, it's what he would have used if he'd had one.)
1	jalapeño (or other chile pepper), chopped (You've probably heard this by now, but a good way to chop hot chile peppers without burning your hands, is to put one hand in a plastic baggie and use that hand to hold the hot chile peppers while you chop.)
½	red sweet pepper, chopped in slivers
¼	cup chopped Italian parsley
2 or 3	small summer squash, chopped in slivers

Cook the pasta according to the directions on the package. Drain and keep warm.

Meanwhile, pour the olive oil, Worcestershire sauce, Tabasco sauce, and black pepper into a large skillet. Heat it up good and hot. Sauté the cabbage, carrots, and garlic for a minute or so, then add the onion, hot and sweet peppers, and parsley. When everything is starting to look translucent, add the summer squash. Stir it all for 30 seconds or so, then add the pasta. Continue to stir until everything is well mixed and warm. Serve immediately, and in the words of Federico, *Buon Appetito!* Serves 4

Postscript:

After I'd eaten this wonderful meal and had gotten Federico's recipe, which I had sworn only to reveal if I told his story as well, which I just did, I asked him whatever happened to Ruby? He replied, "The morning after the tattoo, she is gone. No note. No good-bye kiss. This can only mean one thing. Someday she is returning."

Well, I've had a few of those fantasies myself, and in my case, with one special dark-haired exception, I'm glad that's all they were. But, fifteen years later, in 1984, I got a letter from Federico. All that was in the envelope was a Polaroid photo of his right bicep. Tattooed on it was a heart, with the words, "Ruby, El Paso 1984."

Ray Benson

Brenda Ladd

For more than a quarter of a century, Ray Benson has been the lead singer and guitar player for six-time Grammy award winner Asleep At The Wheel. Ray's hard work and engaging nature are credited with keeping the ultimate Texas band in tune with a unique fusion of country, boogie, jazz, blues, rock, Cajun, and western swing after most bands had long disintegrated. A Philadelphia native, Benson moved the Wheel to Austin in 1974—a musician's kind of town, laid back and tolerant. Today Benson lives in Austin with his wife, Diane, and two children, Sam and Aaron. His pet cause is the Wild Basin Wilderness Preserve in Travis County.

The Wheel's Corn Soup

2	tablespoons cornstarch
6–8	cups whole milk
1	medium-sized onion, peeled and chopped
1	garlic clove, minced
¾	cup butter
2	teaspoons chili powder
2	teaspoons ground cumin
1	teaspoon garlic powder
½	teaspoon black pepper
1	teaspoon salt or to taste
4	cups fresh or frozen corn
½	cup masa harina
3–4	green chiles, chopped
	Cheddar or Monterey Jack cheese, shredded for garnish
	Mexican picante salsa or pico de gallo for garnish
	tortilla chips for garnish

Dissolve cornstarch in 1 cup of the milk and set aside.

In a large saucepan or soup pot, sauté onion and garlic in butter over medium heat until soft and translucent, about 5 minutes. Lower heat, add spices, and stir.

Add corn and simmer for 3–5 minutes. Transfer soup to a blender or food processor and purée. While machine is puréeing, add reserved cup of dissolved cornstarch and milk. Pour puréed mixture back into soup pot. Sprinkle masa harina over soup mixture, stir in, and add remaining milk. Bring to low boil over medium heat, stirring occasionally. Add green chiles, lower heat, and simmer for 10 minutes more, stirring frequently.

To serve: Pour hot soup into ovenproof serving bowls. Top with shredded cheese. Place in oven under hot broiler just long enough to melt cheese. Do not brown cheese. Top with picante salsa or pico de gallo and serve with chips. Serves 6

Bevo

Bevo Tackles Pork

The sweet and smoky flavors of the ancho and chipotle chiles lend this roast a rich barbecue taste. Canned chipotle chiles in adobo sauce and ancho chiles are available at most grocery stores. The chiles lose some of their fire when cooked, so don't be too concerned if the raw marinade is very picante.

1   3½-pound boneless pork loin

Marinade:
- 1 cup apple juice
- 3 ancho chiles, seeded
- 3 canned chipotle chiles, seeded, plus 2 teaspoons adobo sauce
- 3 garlic cloves
- 1 tablespoon olive oil
- 1 teaspoon granulated sugar
- 1 teaspoon ground cumin
- 1 teaspoon dry thyme
- ½ teaspoon dry oregano
- 1 teaspoon salt

Using a fork, pierce the pork roast all over. Place in a large bowl or nonreactive pan.

To prepare marinade: In a small sauce pan, bring apple juice and ancho chiles to a boil. Remove from heat and allow to sit for 20 minutes. Transfer to a blender, add chipotle chiles, adobo sauce, garlic, olive oil, sugar, and seasonings. Purée.

Pour marinade over pork. Allow to marinate in refrigerator for at least 6 hours, or overnight. Turn occasionally.

Preheat oven to 350°. Place the pork in a roasting pan, baste with half the marinade, reserving the remaining marinade. Cover roast with aluminum foil and bake for 45 minutes. Remove aluminum foil, baste with remaining marinade, and cook, until the internal temperature reads 150°–160°, about another 45 minutes.

Remove from oven and let roast rest for 10 minutes before carving. Serves 6–8

Texans may love the sports arena more than they love their venerable barbecue sauce. And, sports fans at the University of Texas love their mascot Bevo as much as they love the game of football itself. The 1,500-pound beast comes from a long line of Texas longhorns beginning in 1916. The current Bevo is the 13th generation bovine to strut his stuff at Texas Memorial Stadium. Bevo is considered by many to be just as famous as other UT alumni such as Bill Moyers, Janis Joplin, and Walter Cronkite. Despite his fame, Bevo remains a mascot you can count on, unlike the fuzzy, costumed fake variety.

Architect Sinclair Black has been a major influence in the design of Austin's buildings and the planning of its neighborhoods. While the city has struggled with redevelopment and growth, thanks to citizens like Sinclair, Austin's silhouette is filling in with striking examples of modern architecture and it has retained an easy-living culture between the expressways. Sinclair produced Austin Creeks, a plan to integrate and expand Austin's hiking and biking trails into the fabric of the musical city. He is currently working on a project to improve the streetscapes of the Drag area near the UT campus. Sinclair and his partner, Andrew Vernooy, have truly improved the quality of life in Austin. Their work has garnered numerous design awards and has been widely published and exhibited.

Sinclair Black

Chutney Lime Chicken

Sinclair Black and his wife, Susan Morehead, discovered the inspiration for this dish on a trip to the wine country of California. It its original form, the chicken breasts were grilled over mesquite and served with lime butter and chutney sauce. This revised version not only tastes as good, but it also provides enough chutney lime sauce to serve over rice.

4	boneless, skinless chicken breasts
2–3	fresh limes, juiced
2	tablespoons chopped fresh ginger
6	tablespoons butter, divided
¾	cup Major Grey's chutney

Rinse the chicken and pat dry. Combine the fresh lime juice with the ginger. Marinate the chicken breasts in lime-ginger juice for 30 minutes. Reserve juice.

Heat 2 tablespoons of the butter in a large skillet. Add the chicken breasts, and sauté over medium heat until browned and cooked through, about 4–5 minutes per side. Remove chicken from skillet and keep warm.

To the skillet, add the remaining 4 tablespoons butter, the reserved lime-ginger juice, and the chutney. Whisk together and heat through until thickened, about 3–4 minutes. Serve the chutney sauce over the chicken, and rice, if desired. Serves 4

Boerne Village Band

German Pioneer Whole Wheat Bread

This German bread is not available in grocery stores, but is made often in homes in the Texas Hill Country. —Rudolf Scheffrahn, band member

- 7 cups very warm water
- 1 cup all-purpose unbleached flour
- ½ cup vegetable oil
- ½ cup molasses syrup
- 1 heaping tablespoon salt
- 2 packages active dry yeast
- 5 pounds (17 cups) whole wheat flour

Preheat oven to 200° or lowest setting. Oil 6 loaf pans.

In a extra large mixing bowl, mix water, all-purpose flour, oil, molasses, salt, and yeast. Gradually add half the whole wheat flour (approximately 8½ cups). Stir until smooth. *No rush please.*

Put this dough in an oiled bowl, toss dough to cover all surfaces. Cover and place in warm oven and let rise 30–45 minutes until doubled in bulk. Remove and knead the rest of the remaining whole wheat flour into it. *Take your time, add a good helping of elbow grease and assure a firm, smooth dough.*

Place in oiled bowl, tossing to coat dough surfaces and allow to rise in oven for another 30–45 minutes or until dough has doubled. Divide dough into six portions and form dough to fill prepared pans. Place dough in pans and into warmed oven, allowing another 20 minutes for rising.

Take bread out of oven while you increase oven temperature to 350°. Bake loaves for approximately 70 minutes, rotating pans from front to back once. Loaves should be nicely browned and sound hollow when tapped with the knuckles. Enjoy warm or cool and freeze extra loaves in plastic bags. Makes 6 loaves

Founded in 1860 in the Hill Country town of Boerne by immigrant Karl Dienger, the Boerne Village Band is the oldest German band in the world outside of Deutschland. Just as it has for more than 130 years, the band still entertains in the town's bandstand on summer nights. The Boerne Village Band has received many awards. In 1991, it was honored by the Texas House of Representatives, and in 1996 the Federal Republic of Germany presented the band with its highest award for folk music, the "Pro Musika-Plakette." Keeping the tradition alive, the present band's leader, veterinarian Kenneth Herbst, is the grandson and nephew of former band leaders.

Doyle Bramhall

Good and Healthy Chicken Broth

This recipe was given to me by my friend, Jennifer Warnes. The protein in the broth goes into your bone marrow and helps to create new red blood cells. Great for colds and flu and for anyone suffering from any acute or chronic illness. For the best tasting broth, use only the freshest, natural chicken, organic vegetables and other ingredients. I sometimes add another whole chicken breast, up to 6 cloves garlic and twice the ginger called for in the recipe for a richer flavor. Besides a hot drink, this broth is an excellent base for a noodle and/or vegetable soup. —Doyle Bramhall

2	gallons good water (I use distilled)
1	good quality chicken breast with bone and without skin
4–6	medium-sized carrots, sliced
½	bunch celery, leaves included, chopped
1	bunch parsley
1	small piece fresh ginger (about 2 inches by ¼ inch)
1	garlic clove, do not peel

Important: No salt, pepper or seasonings of any kind.
Place all ingredients in a large kettle and bring to boil. With the lid on, boil for 2½–3 hours. Cool, strain, and throw out everything but the broth.
Drink three times a day. Makes about 2 gallons

Born in Dallas and raised in Irving, Doyle Bramhall grew up listening to everything from country to rhythm and blues to pop. He took up the drums at 14, and two years later, joined the Chessmen, which would soon include Jimmie Vaughan on guitar. In 1970, Bramhall and members of the by then-Texas Storm moved to Austin as part of the great migration of Dallas musicians who would help turn the capital city into a hotbed of American music. He has long been recognized as the man who wrote or co-wrote many of the most memorable tunes in the Stevie Ray Vaughan songbook, including *Tightrope*, *The House Is Rockin'*, and *Hard to Be*. His debut album, *Bird Nest on the Ground*, reveals a singer of rare soulfulness, a writer of depth and directness, and a man with vision and talent. Doyle finds inspiration at home in Wimberley.

Broken Spoke

The Broken Spoke's Chicken Fried Steak with Cream Gravy

Willie Nelson and Randy Travis love it and so do another 800 or so people who order chicken fried steak every week at Austin's legendary honky-tonk.

1	cup buttermilk
1	large egg, beaten
	salt and pepper to taste
½	cup all-purpose flour
½	cup saltine cracker meal
4	3–5 ounce beef cutlets
1	cup shortening

Gravy:
½	cup meat drippings
¼	cup flour
2½	cups milk
	salt and pepper to taste

To prepare the cutlet: Blend the buttermilk, egg, and salt and pepper in a medium mixing bowl. In a separate shallow bowl or plate, blend the flour and cracker meal. Pat both sides of each cutlet with the flour mixture. Then submerge the cutlet in egg-milk mixture and back into the flour mixture, patting both sides again to evenly coat. (This is called double breading and is one reason why the Broken Spoke's chicken fried steak is so good.) Repeat with remaining cutlets.

Meanwhile, heat shortening in a heavy skillet to 325°. Fry cutlets, one at a time, turning until both sides of steak are golden in color. Lift the cutlet out and let excess oil drain off. Place steaks on warm plates.

To prepare the gravy: Drain off all but ¼ cup of drippings and return to medium heat. Gradually stir in flour, and cook until it is golden. Slowly stir in milk, and season with salt and pepper. Spoon gravy over warm cutlet, adding enough for sopping with a dinner roll or slice of white bread. Serves 4

Merilyn Brown

It's not fancy. A rustic, red building and a dirt parking lot. But it damn sure is country. People come from all over the world to have something good to eat and to have a good time at Austin's Broken Spoke. Bob Wills and the Texas Playboys, Don Walser, Willie Nelson, George Strait and Alvin Crow have all played here. The legendary honky-tonk has been featured in *National Geographic*, the *New York Times*, and on the *Today*, show to name a few. James and Annetta White opened it in 1964, and are still running it. James is a fifth-generation Texan (his great uncle was Texas Ranger James Campbell "Doc" White), and he says "Texas means the world" to him.

William Broyles Jr.

Most screenwriters live in Los Angeles. The man who co-wrote the Oscar-winning *Apollo 13* has the clout and resume to live anywhere he chooses: but, he picked Austin. William Broyles Jr. brings a rich and varied background to his typewriter. An alumnus of both Rice and Oxford universities, and a civil-rights activist who served in Vietnam, Bill was a founding editor of *Texas Monthly*, a winner of the National Magazine Award under his leadership. After a time as editor-in-chief at *Newsweek*, Bill vowed he would "never hold a job again." Officially unemployed since 1984, he hasn't been without work. He co-created the television series *China Beach*, winner of four Emmy awards, and is a contributing editor to *Esquire*. Bill is married to Andrea and says they've got "two great kids."

Chicken Kale Soup

Bill's wife, Andrea, submits this recipe. She says it's great for re-heating and freezing.

1	small chicken
1–2	garlic cloves, minced
3	medium potatoes, peeled and chopped into 1-inch pieces
3	bunches kale, stems removed, leaves washed, and chopped
1	bunch parsley, stems removed, leaves washed, and chopped
2	chicken bouillon cubes, or more to taste

Place the chicken in a large stock pot, and fill with water until chicken is covered. Bring to a boil and simmer the chicken for 45 minutes. Remove chicken from pot and set aside. Skim off any foam and fat from the surface.

To the stock, add the garlic, potatoes, kale, parsley, and bouillon cubes. Cover and simmer over medium heat for 30 minutes.

Meanwhile, debone the chicken and shred the meat. Add the chicken meat to the stock, and heat through. Serves 8

Janelle Buchanan

Greenbelt Chicken and Brown Rice Salad

My Chicken and Brown Rice Salad is very easy to make, travels well, and can be served at room temperature or chilled. Thus, it's a great dish for a picnic at Barton Springs or on the Greenbelt. —Janelle Buchanan

- ¾ cup mayonnaise
- 1 tablespoon lemon juice
- ¼ teaspoon salt
- ½ teaspoon curry powder, or more to taste
- ½ teaspoon tarragon, or more to taste
- 2 cups cooked, cubed chicken
- 2 cups cooked brown rice
- 1 cup slivered celery stalks
- 1 4-ounce can sliced water chestnuts, drained
- ¼ cup sliced green onion
- ¼ cup slivered, toasted almonds

In a small bowl, combine the mayonnaise, lemon juice, salt, curry powder, and tarragon. Whisk together.

In a large Tupperware bowl, combine the chicken, brown rice, celery, water chestnuts, and green onion. Pour the dressing over, and mix well. Top with slivered almonds. Chill for several hours before serving or transporting to a park. Serves 4–6

Janelle Buchanan has been a leading lady on the Austin theater scene for over a decade, starring in such productions as *Our Town*, *A Midsummer Night's Dream*, and *Death and the Maiden*. Janelle played a dime dancer in Clint Eastwood's *A Perfect World*, and has appeared in numerous television commercials. Janelle provided the voice of Mrs. Spottish in the gruesome *Texas Chainsaw Massacre III*. She is proud of her many roles as a five-year member of Zachary Scott Theatre Center's Project InterAct, a company of adult professional actors performing for children at Austin's oldest theater. Janelle is married to Ted Siff, the director of the Texas field office of the Trust for Public Lands.

Bob Bullock

Bob Bullock rarely sleeps, but when he does it's with one eye open. Or so it would appear to those who monitor Texas politics. Bob, lieutenant governor since 1991, knows and sees everything that goes on in the capital city and beyond. His political savvy and network of allies come from years of service to his beloved state—as secretary of state, assistant attorney general, and as a member of the Texas House of Representatives. A native of Hillsboro, Texas, Bob has lived in Austin since 1967. In the rare times Bob does take a break from public life, he kicks back at his 200-acre ranch near Llano with his wife Jan, an interior designer.

Brown Beans by Bullock

It shouldn't be necessary to have a recipe for cooking a pot of pinto beans. But it must be. I've come to that conclusion after the many times I've been served mushy pintos that don't even deserve to be recycled on a nacho.

Soaking the beans overnight is the Number One Killer of a good pot of beans. Don't do it. This old soaking-overnight-mistake is a hangover from the days when beans were sold in bulk straight from the fields without washing. Today's packaged beans are free from dirt and rocks and need only a little rinsing.

The second enemy of a good pot of pintos is cooking them too long in the name of making them just soft enough to eat. How *long* they cook isn't the answer—*how* they cook is. Put your beans in a pot and cover them at least three times higher with water. Bring to a rapid boil for five minutes covered. After five minutes of boiling, turn out the fire and DO NOT OPEN THE LID. If you open the lid, forget it. You've ruined it.

Let the covered pot set for one hour. Then turn the fire back on just a little higher than a simmer. When the pot starts boiling again and the lid starts jumping around and sputtering over on the stove, put in a tablespoon of oil. This will cut down the sputtering.

After a couple of hours—a little longer if you're busy doing something else—you should need to add more water. Add only *hot* water. Never put cold water into boiling food.

This is also a good time to add some onion, a slab of pork, or whatever else you like. The salt pork sold in most markets today is so sorry that you get about the same good out of a couple strips of bacon.

Now turn the fire down to simmer, and thicken the juice. A tablespoon or two of brown sugar works fine. It doesn't taste in the beans. Some folks like to use two or three tablespoons of masa flour worked into a paste. You can taste this in the beans—but it is good. Incidentally, if you don't keep masa flour around, you can get the same effect by pulverizing a handful of Fritos.

Now the beans can simmer until they are exactly like you want them. They will not get mushy. At this point you can also decide if you want just plain beans or if you want to go another route. If you like something off in the sweet direction, put in some more brown sugar or a little molasses.

If you want something with a little zing, put in whatever is your favorite barbecue sauce, steak sauce, chili powder, jalapeños, or the like.

When all this is simmering in good, you're ready to eat. If you're planning ahead, you can now put the beans in the icebox and warm 'em up when ready. Just warm them; don't cook 'em to death. They won't get mushy, but the juice will get thick. Good eating!

Barbara & George Bush

Fabulous Noodle Kugel

This is one of the Bush family's most popular recipes and was supplied by friend Elaine Wynn. Note that this recipe makes enough for a large family gathering.

1	pound wide egg noodles, cooked
1	cup granulated sugar
1	pound cottage cheese
1½	teaspoons vanilla
1	cup white raisins
7	eggs, beaten
3	cups milk
1	pint sour cream
½	cup butter, melted
	cinnamon and salt, to taste
	Corn Flakes for topping
¼	cup butter, cut in small cubes

Mix all ingredients (except Corn Flakes and cubed butter) in a large bowl. Pour into large baking pan and refrigerate overnight, or for at least 3 hours.

Before serving, preheat oven to 350°. Cover noodles mixture with Corn Flakes, and dot with butter. Bake for 1½ hours or until golden brown. Serves 15–20

In 1948, when Barbara and George were newly married, the couple left their families and the familiarity of New England for the vast open lands and opportunities of Texas. Barbara often credits that move for forcing them to grow up quickly and for solidifying their marriage. With Barbara at his side, George established a petroleum corporation, ran for the U.S. Senate, was elected to the U.S. House of Representatives, became ambassador to the United Nations and director of the CIA, ran with Ronald Reagan, and of course the rest is familiar history. While the Bushes occasionally retreat on family vacations to their Maine compound in Kennebunkport, Texas remains their home.

George W. Bush

He was called "George the Younger," "The First Son," and "The Shrub." Now they call him *Governor*. George W. Bush is the quick-witted, articulate, savvy politician who beat out one of the most popular governors in Texas history. As governor, he has worked successfully with the legislature to implement four of his campaign promises—to reform education, welfare, tort litigation, and juvenile justice. Despite an Ivy League education (George graduated from both Yale University and Harvard Business School), he is a country person at heart. He leans toward a more casual atmosphere at the office, where he's been known to greet visitors in a baseball cap with country music playing in the background. He and his wife, Laura, a former public school librarian, have twin daughters, Barbara and Jenna, who were named for their grandmothers.

Statehouse Pecan Pie

Pecan Pie is one of my favorite desserts. I hope you enjoy it as much as I do. I warn you—it is not dietetic. Desserts like this one keep me jogging every day. —George W. Bush

1½	cups Texas pecan halves
1	9-inch pie shell
3	eggs
1	tablespoon butter, at room temperature
1	cup dark corn syrup
½	teaspoon vanilla
1	cup granulated sugar
1	tablespoon all-purpose flour

Preheat oven to 350°.

Arrange the pecan halves in the pie shell and set aside. In a mixing bowl, beat the eggs until light. Add the butter, corn syrup, and vanilla. Stir until well blended. In a separate mixing bowl, combine the sugar and flour. Fold the dry ingredients into the wet ingredients. Pour the mixture over the pecan halves, and let sit until the pecans rise to the surface. Bake for 45 minutes. Serve warm or at room temperature. Serves 8

Laura Bush

Blueberry Sweet Potato Bread

When it comes to sharing a great meal with friends and family, George and I most enjoy planning "Totally Texas" events. The Governor's Mansion's chefs, Sarah Bishop and Kathy Russell, or celebrity chefs who we've invited to join us, prepare meals using Texas foods and ingredients, which have enormous variety and appeal. I submit the Texas School Recipe Roundup Contest's winning recipe, created by Faye Porter. We tried this fabulous dessert during our "Totally Texas" lunch in April.

From a fabulous array of food and decorations, to a host of artistic talent, we are fortunate to have so much to share with our friends—and it's all made in Texas. Thank you for supporting the Austin Parks Foundation. —Laura Bush

- 2 cups all-purpose flour
- 1 tablespoon baking powder
- ¼ teaspoon baking soda
- ¾ tablespoon cinnamon
- ¼ teaspoon nutmeg
- 1 cup granulated sugar
- 1 cup boiled fresh sweet potatoes, mashed
- 2 tablespoons sweet potato liquid
- 2 large eggs, beaten
- ¼ cup vegetable oil
- 1 cup blueberries

Spray a 9x5x3-inch loaf pan with non-stick vegetable cooking spray. Preheat oven to 350°.

In a small bowl, stir together the flour, baking powder, baking soda, cinnamon, and nutmeg. Set aside. In a larger bowl, by hand, combine the sugar, sweet potatoes, liquid, eggs, and oil. Mix well. Add the flour mixture to the sweet potato mixture, stirring until just moistened. Fold in the blueberries. Pour the batter into the loaf pan and bake for 60 minutes, or until a toothpick inserted in the center comes out clean. Remove bread from pan and cool on wire rack. For optimal flavor, bake the bread a day before serving and wrap in plastic overnight. Makes 1 loaf

"When I married Laura, she was a shy librarian whose idea of oratory was Shhhh! Now that she has become such a good speaker and is becoming so loved by those who meet her, the same thing that happened to my old man has happened to me," George W. Bush said of his wife. Indeed, Texans see in Laura Bush the same sense of grace and authentic finesse that Americans saw in her mother-in-law, Barbara Bush. And, like the former First Lady, Laura has used her position to champion one of her favorite causes—literacy. In 1995, Laura Bush announced the creation of the Texas Book Festival, which brings Texan writers such as Larry McMurtry, Mary Karr, and William Wittliff to Austin for readings and signings, and to benefit Texas libraries. In the words of the First Lady, the festival is intended to "nourish our souls."

Earl Campbell

Earl Campbell's Sausage Jambalaya

Spice Mix:
- 1 teaspoon salt
- ½ teaspoon freshly ground black pepper
- ½ teaspoon ground cayenne pepper
- ½ teaspoon ground white pepper
- 1 teaspoon dry mustard
- ½ teaspoon dried thyme leaf

- 1½ cups chopped onion
- 1 cup chopped green bell pepper
- 1½ cups chopped celery
- 1½ teaspoons minced garlic cloves
- 4 tablespoons margarine
- 1 pound Earl Campbell's smoked sausage, cut into 1-inch slices
- 2 cups long-grain white rice
- 4 cups chicken stock
- 4 small bay leaves

The rose capital of the world unveiled its most fruitful rose ever on March 28, 1955, when Earl Campbell was born in Tyler, Texas. Earl's legendary football career may have budded in Tyler, but it blossomed at the University of Texas, where he was awarded the Heisman Trophy and was twice named an All-American. After college, Earl's accomplishments as a running back with the Houston Oiler's earned him several MVP and All-Pro titles. In recognition of his achievements, the Texas State Legislature named Earl Campbell the fourth official State Hero of Texas. Still, Earl considers his bachelor's degree in speech communication earned at UT in 1978 his most prized possession. Today, he speaks at 150 engagements a year on such wide-ranging topics as golf, hunting, panic disorder, and education. Earl lives in Austin with his wife, high-school sweetheart Reuna, and their two sons.

In a small bowl, combine the spice mix ingredients. Mix well and set aside. In a separate bowl, combine the onion, bell pepper, celery, and garlic and set aside.

Heat the margarine in a large heavy skillet over medium-high heat. Add the sausage and cook for 5–7 minutes, stirring occasionally. Add the vegetable mixture and the spice mix. Cook until well browned, about 10–12 minutes more. Stir occasionally, scraping the bottom of the pan.

Add the rice, and mix well with the meat and vegetables. Stirring occasionally, cook the rice for 5 minutes. Add the chicken stock and bay leaves, and mix together. Bring the mixture to a boil, reduce heat, and simmer until rice is just tender, about 20 minutes. Remove bay leaves and serve. Serves 4

Sarah Elizabeth Campbell

Bummer Summer Salad

I stole this recipe from Julie Speed. —Sarah Elizabeth Campbell

Dressing:
- 3½ tablespoons honey
- 3½ tablespoons toasted sesame oil
- 5 tablespoons balsamic vinegar
- 1 tablespoon finely chopped red onion
- salt and freshly ground black pepper to taste

- 4–5 garlic cloves, minced
- 1 cup finely chopped fresh basil
- 1 15-ounce can sweet corn, drained
- 1 11-ounce can mandarin oranges, drained
- fresh garden greens
- feta cheese, optional

In a small bowl, mix the dressing ingredients together, and set aside.

In another bowl, combine the garlic, fresh basil, and sweet corn. Toss lightly with the dressing, and chill.

Before serving, fold in the mandarin oranges. Be gentle with them—it's their last time. That's the only bummer. Arrange the garden greens on a large platter, and spoon the sweet corn-mandarin mixture over the greens. Add a little feta cheese, if you want to be bad. Serves 2–4

Brenda Ladd Photography

Sarah Elizabeth Campbell grew up around the Austin music scene of the 1970s and started performing as a teenager. She recalls, "When I was sixteen, most of my friends were in their 20s and 30s, and Marcia Ball was my idol." Awestruck by what she saw, she decided early that singing and writing songs was what she wanted to do for a living. And, she has done just that. Sarah has released two albums, *Running With You* and *A Little Tenderness*, both of which have seen wide acceptance in a harsh industry. One of her original songs found its way onto the *Threadgill's Supper Session Second Helping* compilation, which illuminates some of the local heroes of the rich Austin musical landscape.

Eugene Cernan

As commander of Apollo XVII, Eugene Cernan holds the unique distinction of being the last man to have left his footprints on the lunar surface. He was also the second American to walk in space with the Gemini IX mission. He says, "Once you walk on the moon, you can never unwalk it," and he has been involved in the space business ever since. Presently, his Cernan Corporation consults with and assists aerospace engineering companies that work with NASA's space center in Houston. While he's thrilled to be in the middle of the highest flying industry in America, Eugene's ideal is more down to earth. He says that he would rather spend time on his Bigwood Springs Ranch south of Kerrville. There, he raises longhorns, horses, and several exotics.

The Ultimate Chicken Spaghetti

A great one-pot meal that saves on cleanup but does not sacrifice taste.

2	pounds chicken breasts
1	medium onion, chopped
2	garlic cloves, chopped
2	tablespoon fresh parsley, chopped, or 1 tablespoon dried parsley
½	teaspoon ground black pepper
1	tablespoon granulated sugar
1	tablespoon dried sweet basil
1	teaspoon salt
⅓	cup olive oil
4	6-ounce cans tomato paste
2	cups water
1	pound spaghetti, cooked

Sauté chicken and chopped onion in the olive oil in a large, heavy pot over medium heat, until chicken is browned, about 5–7 minutes. Add garlic, parsley, pepper, sugar, basil, and salt. Stir well to coat chicken with seasonings and cover. Lower heat and cook slowly, stirring occasionally, for about 20 minutes. Add tomato paste and water, stirring well. Simmer for about 45 minutes until the sauce is thickened and chicken is tender. (If sauce needs to thicken more, lift chicken out with slotted spoon and simmer sauce about 15 minutes more.)

Serve chicken and sauce over spaghetti. Serves 6

Fran Christina

Jane's Drunken Chicken 'n' Dumplins

A good friend of ours, Janet Anthenien, catered the recording of the Thunderbirds' 1984 album **T-Bird Rhythm** *at the now-defunct Third Coast Studios in Austin. The mix just wasn't right until I spilled a bowl of Jane's Chicken and Dumplings into the mixing board. It also worked great for sopping up tequila. —Fran Christina*

1	5-pound chicken hen	Dumplings:	
1	onion, chopped	2	cups flour, divided
3	celery stalks, finely chopped	1	tablespoon baking powder
1	bay leaf	½	teaspoon salt
1	tablespoon finely chopped fresh thyme leaves, or a pinch of dried	1	egg
	salt and pepper to taste	2	tablespoons butter, melted
1	cup dry vermouth	½	cup milk
¼	cup butter, at room temperature	¼	cup butter, at room temperature
¼	cup all-purpose flour	½	bunch Italian parsley, stems removed and finely chopped
		¼	teaspoon freshly ground black pepper

  Place the chicken in a large pot with the onion, celery, bay leaf, thyme, salt and pepper, and vermouth. Add enough water to cover the chicken by two inches. Bring to a boil, reduce heat, and simmer until chicken is tender, about 1½ hours. Remove chicken and set aside. Continue cooking the stock, uncovered, until it is reduced to 6 cups, about 15 minutes more. Skim any fat or froth from the stock, and reserve the stock in the pot.
  Meanwhile, to make the dumplings: Sift 1¾ cups flour, baking powder, and salt together in a large bowl. In a small bowl, beat the egg, melted butter, and milk together. Gradually add the wet ingredients to the dry ingredients, and stir until just moistened. Sprinkle the remaining ¼ cup flour onto a flat surface and knead the dough until elastic. Roll the dough out on the floured surface to a quarter-inch thickness. Spread the softened butter over the dough and sprinkle with the parsley and black pepper. Cut dough into 1- to 2-inch strips. Set aside.
  Bring the chicken stock to a simmer, but do not boil. In a small bowl, mix together the remaining ¼ cup flour and ¼ cup butter. Add this to the stock, whisking until the stock is thickened and smooth. Gently drop the dumpling strips into the stock few at a time, stirring as needed. Cover tightly and simmer on low heat for 45 minutes.
  Meanwhile, remove the meat from the chicken bones. After the dumplings are cooked, add the chicken meat, and heat through. Let stand for 15 minutes before serving in bowls. Serves 6

Tracy Hart

Fran Christina pounds on a set of drums as fast and rhythmically as the beat of a hummingbird's heart. The blues percussionist has had plenty of practice. Fran was a founding member of the rock- and blues-driven band, Roomful of Blues, and he has toured or recorded with numerous stars, including Asleep at the Wheel, Bonnie Raitt, Junior Brown, Stevie Ray Vaughan, and Carlos Santana. Fran joined The Fabulous Thunderbirds in 1979, and his friend Kim Wilson says, "Fran's been there all along, giving this band an unshakable foundation, and he's a solid friend. That's what the T-Birds are all about." Fran is married to Austin artist Julie Speed.

Chuy's

Chuy's Tex-Mex Chili Con Carne

Chili Con Carne is at the heart of classic Tex-Mex cooking. The chili queen street vendors of San Antonio originally developed this recipe at the old Military Plaza circa 1890. This sauce is recommended for cheese or beef enchiladas. It is also great on tamales or as an ingredient in a lively cheese omelet.

10	dried guajillo or cascabel chiles
4	ancho or pasilla chiles
1	pound lean coarsely ground sirloin
1	cup chopped onion
4	cups beef stock, preferably homemade
2	teaspoons minced garlic
3	tablespoons tomato paste
2	teaspoons ground cumin
½	teaspoon salt
1	tablespoon flour
1	tablespoon butter

Clean the chiles and remove the stems and seeds. Preheat oven to 300°. Put the chiles on a cookie sheet and toast in the oven for 2–3 minutes. Do not overcook or burn. Put the chiles in a small saucepan with enough water to just cover. Bring to a boil, and immediately remove from the heat.

Let the chiles sit and rehydrate for 10–15 minutes. Put the chile and water into a blender, and purée until smooth. Pour the chile mixture through a fine sieve to collect the pulp. Discard pulp and set chile mixture aside.

In a large skillet, brown the ground sirloin, onion, and garlic. Drain off any fat. Add the puréed chile mixture, beef stock, tomato paste, cumin, and salt to the beef.

Make a roux of the flour and butter by browning them together in a sauté pan over medium heat until the mixture is a deep brown color, about 10–15 minutes. Add the roux to the beef mixture. Bring to a boil, and mix well to fully incorporate the roux into the beef. Lower heat and simmer for 20–30 minutes, or until the sauce reaches a light gravy consistency. Makes 2 quarts

---

Despite having failed at one eatery, partners Mike Young and John Zapp just couldn't give up their dream of owning a successful restaurant. Still heavily in debt, they opened the first Chuy's in the early 1980s. Some might have called the restaurant humble, others might have called it tacky. After all, it was once a very run-down barbecue joint with a dusty dirt parking lot out front and a men's room out back. But the funky decor and low-priced Tex-Mex cuisine caught on. And eventually, the parking lot was paved, the men's room moved inside, and several more restaurants opened across the state. Apparently, Young and Zapp haven't forgotten their meager beginnings. Every year before Christmas, Chuy's sponsors a parade. But the Santa at this parade doesn't hand out gifts, this Santa collects gifts, which are then distributed to less-fortunate children.

Jody Conradt

Slam Dunk Oatmeal Cookies

This recipe was dictated to me by my grandmother more than three decades ago in the midst of a "sweet fit." She served these cookies to the kids in Goldthwaite, and they were great on hot summer days with a wash-down of iced tea or lemonade. Grandma knew I spent most of my time with sports, so this short, sweet, simple recipe remains trustworthy for one who doesn't get to spend much time in the kitchen—and who still experiences sweet fits. —Jody Conradt

- ¾ cup all-purpose flour
- ½ teaspoon baking soda
- ½ teaspoon salt
- ½ cup packed brown sugar
- ½ cup granulated sugar
- ½ cup butter, at room temperature
- 1 egg, beaten
- ½ teaspoon vanilla extract
- ½ cup quick rolled-oats
- ¼ cup chopped nuts

In a large mixing bowl, combine all of the ingredients together. Mix well. Shape the dough into an oblong roll. Roll the dough in wax paper to seal. Keep dough in the ice box until ready to use.

To make the cookies: Preheat oven to 350°. Slice the dough into rounds (about a teaspoon per cookie) and arrange them, 2 inches apart, on greased baking sheets. Bake for 8–10 minutes. Cool the cookies on wire racks. Makes 4 dozen

Build it and they will come. That dream must has been in the back of Coach Jody Conradt's mind when she began building the women's basketball program at the University of Texas over twenty years ago. Today, basketball enthusiasts—sometimes as many as 12,000 screaming loyal fans—flock to the Frank Erwin Center to watch the Lady Longhorns. The reason they come lies in simple, everyday statistics. Under Jody's swift leadership, the team has ranked among the top ten nationally in the past ten years, including No.1 rankings in 1986 and 1987. Jody averages twenty-eight wins a season, and is the only active women's collegiate coach to achieve more than 600 career wins. But dreams and statistics aside, there are really just two simple reasons for Coach Conradt's overwhelming success: Jody loves basketball and the fans love Jody.

Ben Crenshaw

A Master's Creamed Corn
Slow cook this corn for the most succulent side dish imaginable.

- 6 ears of young tender corn
- ¼ cup butter
- 2 cups milk
- 2 cups half & half
- salt and pepper to taste.

With a sharp knife, cut corn from ears and scrape the "milk" from the ears into a bowl. In a large heavy skillet, melt butter over low heat and add corn and its milk. Gently stir in milk and half & half. Simmer gently for 2–3 hours, stirring frequently. Season with salt and pepper. Serves 4–6

"When you grow up with Tom Kite in the same town, and you play against him from the age of ten on, it's bound to help." Ben Crenshaw credits Austin's fiercely competitive spirit and the instruction he received from his longtime friend, golf guru Harvey Penick, for shaping him into a world-class golfer. While Ben played football, basketball, and baseball in high school, golf already had its hooks into him. At the University of Texas, he captured many amateur championships before turning pro in 1973. A string of victories in major tournaments followed, but none have been as sweet as the 1995 Masters championship, which Ben played in honor of Harvey, who had recently died. Dubbed "Gentle Ben" for his easy-going manner both on and off the golf links, Ben spends much of his time designing golf courses around the world, including Austin's own Barton Springs Country Club.

Roberta Crenshaw

Goodie Bars

Good doesn't go far enough to describe these scrumptious, chewy, rich, caramel-flavored, pecan-studded jewels. Yum. If you want something sweet that the whole family will go nuts over, cook these and enjoy the raves.

- 2 cups all-purpose flour
- 2 cups dark brown sugar, packed
- 1 cup granulated sugar
- 1 teaspoon salt
- 1 teaspoon baking powder
- 1 cup butter, melted
- 4 eggs
- 1½ cups pecans, chopped
- 2 tablespoons powdered sugar

Preheat oven to 350°.

Mix dry ingredients in a large mixing bowl. Add melted butter. Add eggs, one at a time, stirring after each one with wooden spoon until all dry ingredients are moist and mixture is smooth. Stir in pecans.

Spread mixture evenly into a lightly greased 13x9-inch pan. Bake for 35–45 minutes. Remove from oven and dust with powdered sugar. Cool and cut into squares.
Makes 24 bars

If one person can be credited with advancing parks and making Austin a great place to live, Roberta "Bobbie" Crenshaw would have to be the one. In the '40s, Bobbie bought 389 trees, peaches, jasmine and weeping willows, and she and other volunteers planted them along Town Lake, starting at Congress Avenue and stretching to Lamar. At the same time, the volunteers carved out the very first Austin hiking trail along the river. Later, she was a driving force behind the founding of the Austin Parks and Recreation Department Advisory Board, and became a long-standing board member. Quietly, she bought the land for Reed Park and much of the land for the Colorado River Park and donated it to the city. Bobbie was the impetus behind the creation of Umlauf Gardens. Her generosity and energy have not just been confined to the parks. She has been a leader in the Austin's arts community also.

Elizabeth Crook

A self-ascribed late-comer, Elizabeth Crook came to Austin as an adult. Nonetheless, Austin holds a place in her heart only "home" occupies. The fourth-generation Texan is the author of the bestselling novel *The Raven's Bride*, a study of the ill-fated marriage of Sam Houston to Eliza Allen. In her most recent book, *Promised Lands*, Elizabeth deftly and wryly recounts the events leading up to the massacre of 342 Texan soldiers at the hands of Santa Anna's troops in 1836. Elizabeth's finely tuned sentences and ability to capture the emotion of history have established her as an author to watch in the coming years.

As Promised Texas Pralines

My mother started making these pralines for friends at Christmas forty years ago. She now makes at least twenty batches every year, filling thirty Christmas cans. I have known of times when she was late delivering and friends called up to find out where their pralines were. President Lyndon Johnson loved them and so did Louisiana Senator Ellender, who was famous for his own praline recipe.

These are better than the slick rubbery pralines or the sugary ones in restaurants. If done right, they are as creamy as butter mints. Most cooks do better on the second try. I have never tried myself but I've eaten a lot of them. —Elizabeth Crook

2   cups granulated sugar
1   cup buttermilk
1   teaspoon baking soda
2   cups pecan halves
2   tablespoons butter or margarine

Combine the sugar, buttermilk, and baking soda in large saucepan over medium heat. Bring to a boil, stirring constantly. Boil for five minutes. (Careful: the hot mixture foams, grows, and pops.)

Add pecans and butter and continue to cook, stirring constantly, until a small blob dropped in cold water forms a soft ball (Use a candy thermometer to measure 236°–238°). Remove from heat and beat with a wooden spoon until the mixture holds its shape when dropped by tablespoonfuls onto a waxed paper-lined cookie sheet. Drop the mixture when it begins to turn opaque and starts to harden around the sides of the pan.

The trick to this recipe is knowing when the candy is ready to drop. If it's too hard it turns sugary, if it's too soft it stays sticky. Makes 20 large pralines

Josh Davis

Fat-Freestyle Turkey Chili

1½	pounds ground turkey
1	teaspoon vegetable oil
1	medium onion, chopped
1	8-ounce can tomato sauce
1	14½-ounce can Rotel chopped chiles and tomatoes
1	40-ounce can ranch-style beans
1	tablespoon chili powder
1	teaspoon ground cumin
	picante sauce to taste

In a large stock pot, brown the turkey in the vegetable oil over medium heat, about 5–7 minutes. Add the remaining ingredients and stir together. Cover and simmer for 30 minutes. Add the picante sauce as desired for extra flavor. Serve with rice. Serves 6

Two wonderful things happened to Josh Davis during his years at the University of Texas: Longhorn volleyball player Shantel Cornelius and freestyle swimming excellence. At UT, Josh won Shantel's hand in marriage. He also earned twenty-three All American swimming titles and he was voted "Most Valuable Player" and "Most Spirited" several times by his teammates. Josh went on to become a member of the U.S.A. Olympic Swim Team, bringing home three gold medals from Atlanta. The San Antonio native, who was ranked first in the world in the 200-meter freestyle, now resides in Austin where he enjoys reading the *Bible*, sleeping, and most of all, eating.

Libby Doggett

One person making a difference—that's Libby Belk Doggett, a bona fide force of nature. Under her leadership, Arc of Texas, a statewide, grassroots group dedicated to assisting people with mental retardation and their families, became a stable and productive organization. Libby also founded and chaired the Disability Policy Consortium, a coalition of 20 advocacy organizations that has been a powerful voice for those with disabilities in Texas. She recently co-authored *All Kids Count: Child Care and the Americans with Disabilities Act*. Libby is married to U.S. Representative Lloyd Doggett, and they have two daughters.

Lloyd's Favorite Gingerbread

We eat it with applesauce or sometimes we splurge and use whipped cream. —Libby Doggett

- 3 eggs, well beaten
- 1 cup granulated sugar
- 2 cups all-purpose flour
- 1 teaspoon ground cinnamon
- 1 teaspoon ground ginger
- 1 teaspoon ground cloves
- 1 cup vegetable oil
- 1 cup dark molasses
- 2 teaspoons baking soda, dissolved in 2 tablespoons hot water

Preheat oven to 375°.

In a large mixing bowl, cream together eggs and sugar. Stir in flour and spices. Add oil and molasses, and mix thoroughly. Dissolve soda in hot water and add to batter; stir well. Pour in a greased 13x9-inch baking dish and bake for 30 minutes. Cool. Makes 1 loaf

Robert Draper

Circle J Pumpkin Risotto

If you are preparing this dish during the summer, fresh pumpkin may not be available. Try using Hubbard's squash, or failing that, butternut squash, each of which makes a delicious substitute. —Robert Draper

Broth:
- 6 cups water
- ½ small pumpkin (about 3 pounds in size), roughly chopped
- ½ medium yellow onion, roughly chopped
- 2 carrots, roughly chopped
- 1 bunch fresh thyme leaves, roughly chopped
- salt and pepper to taste

Risotto base:
- the other half of the pumpkin
- 3 tablespoons olive oil
- 2 garlic cloves, minced
- ¼ cup chopped yellow onion
- ¼ cup chopped leeks
- 1½ cups Arborio rice
- 1 cup dry white wine

Garnish:
- ¼ cup chopped fresh sage
- ¼ cup chopped cabbage
- ¼ cup chopped scallions
- ¼ cup freshly grated Romano cheese

To prepare the broth: In a large pot, bring the water to a boil. Add the broth ingredients, and simmer for at least 1 hour. Drain the broth through a fine sieve, reserving the liquid. Discard the vegetables and thyme.

Meanwhile, to prepare the risotto base: Preheat the oven to 400°. Cut the remaining half pumpkin in half again. In a small casserole dish with a ¼ inch of water in the bottom, place the two pumpkin pieces skin-side up. Steam in the oven for 45 minutes. Remove from oven, scoop out and discard the pulp and seeds, and then spoon out the pumpkin meat from the skin. The meat should be soft and mushy. Heat the olive oil in a large skillet over medium heat. Add the garlic, and sauté for 1 minute. Add the onion and leek, and sauté until soft, about 5 minutes. Add the pumpkin, mix well, and sauté for 5 additional minutes. Add the Arborio rice, and stir. Add the wine, and stir constantly until the wine is absorbed. Slowly add the broth, ½ cup at a time, stirring constantly until all of the stock has been added. The risotto should be a thick, creamy consistency. This process should take about 20–25 minutes. Taste the rice, and if it is not yet fully cooked, continue cooking and stirring, using ¼ cup water in place of the broth.

Remove risotto from heat, stir in the garnishes, and serve at once. Serves 6

Robert Draper's instinct for detail was honed at an early age. The Houston-native spent nearly every summer and holidays at his grandfather's 365-acre ranch, the Circle J, outside of Wimberley. There he watched and absorbed the interaction between man and nature, and the nuances of rural life. The surrounding countryside revealed itself to him in subtle ways—from the outline of the hills against a sunset, to the spawning of fish in the creek beds. Indeed, when Robert decided in 1984 to become a freelance writer, it was to the Circle J that he sought solitude and a place to begin a new career. Years later, the Austin resident is now a senior editor at *Texas Monthly* and the author of *Rolling Stone Magazine: The Uncensored History*. A lifelong Texan, Robert is a self-described "gadfly on the Texas culinary scene."

The Driskill

Marinated Portobello Mushrooms with Black Bean Sauce

Chef Ron Brannon sends this recipe from Austin's historic landmark hotel.

Love, history and deceit have made the historic Driskill hotel an Austin landmark. Swept up by the romantic ambiance of The Driskill, a love-struck LBJ proposed to Lady Bird on their first date. And Tommy Lee Jones exchanged wedding vows there. The fate of one of the nation's most significant landmarks, the Alamo, was decided within the walls of The Driskill by the Daughters of the Republic. Texas lawmen set an ambush at the grand hotel for the infamous couple, Bonnie and Clyde. As symbolic of Austin as the Capital and Governor's Mansion, the magnificent Driskill hotel has graced Sixth Street since December 1886. Today it continues as a showcase of true hospitality still found only in the Lone Star state.

Portobello mushroom marinade:
- 1 cup Shiner Bock beer
- 1 tablespoon packed brown sugar
- 1 tablespoon minced yellow onion
- 1½ tablespoons Worcestershire sauce
- ½ teaspoon Tabasco sauce
- ¾ tablespoon Zatarain's mustard
- ¾ tablespoon minced garlic cloves
- ½ teaspoon freshly ground black pepper
- ½ tablespoon Lawry's seasoning salt
- 2 pounds portobello mushrooms

Black bean sauce:
- 2½ ounces bacon, diced
- ⅓ cup diced onion
- 1 teaspoon minced garlic cloves
- 1 cup canned black beans, drained
- 1 poblano chile pepper, seeds removed, roasted, skinned, and diced
- 1 New Mexico chile pepper, seeds removed, roasted, skinned and diced
- ½ tablespoon chopped fresh cilantro
- ¾ cup water
- pinch cumin seeds, toasted

To prepare the portobello mushroom marinade: Whisk all of the marinade ingredients together in a large glass bowl. Wash and remove the stems from the mushrooms. Add the mushrooms to the marinade, cover, and refrigerate at least 6 hours or overnight. Before serving, grill or bake the portobello mushrooms. To bake, arrange the mushrooms in a single layer in a baking dish, and bake at 350° until the mushrooms are tender and browned, about 20 minutes. To grill, place the mushrooms over medium coals, turn frequently, and cook until tender, about 10–15 minutes.

To prepare the black bean sauce: In a medium stock pot, sauté the bacon, onion, and garlic over low heat until the bacon is just barely crisp. Do not let the garlic burn. Drain off fat. Add the black beans, the chile peppers, chopped cilantro, water, and cumin seeds. Bring to a boil, and remove from heat. Puree the black bean mixture, and then push through a fine sieve.

Drizzle the black bean sauce over 6–8 salad plates, and top with the mushrooms. Serve immediately as a side dish or an hors d'oeuvre. Serves 6–8.

Chris Duarte

Shade Tree Banana Pudding

This is a perfect dessert to take to a summer picnic at the park. Everyone, from grandpa to the kids, will delight in its creamy perfection.

¾	cup granulated sugar, divided
⅓	cup all-purpose flour
	dash salt
2	cups milk
4	eggs, separated
½	teaspoon vanilla
5 to 6	bananas, cut into slices
1	box Vanilla Wafers

Preheat oven to 425°.

Combine ½ cup of sugar, flour, and salt in a double boiler. Beat together milk and egg yolks. Pour into sugar mixture in double boiler, whisking until smooth. Bring water in double boiler to rapid boil, and cook pudding, stirring frequently, until mixture has thickened, about 5 minutes. Remove from heat and add vanilla. When cool, add sliced bananas to pudding mixture. Set aside.

In a small mixing bowl, add remaining sugar (¼ cup) to egg whites, and beat until stiff peaks form. Set meringue aside.

In a 2-quart casserole, place a layer of wafers at bottom and sides. Pour in half of banana filling, place another layer of wafers and top with meringue.

Place in preheated oven and cook for about 5 minutes or until the meringue starts to brown. Can be served warm or cool. Serves 6

Kevin Knight

Austin has proven fertile breeding ground for a variety of stylistic mutations of the electric guitar. One of the dominant strains is blues, Texas blues. King, Collins, Winter, and the Vaughans have all been exponents of a style where fire and sting impart the Texas stamp. Add Chris Duarte, who was drawn from his native San Antonio to Austin when he was 16, to the list of greats. His sound is pure, burning emotion. The Chris Duarte Group's debut album, *Texas Sugar/Strat Magik*, is like blowing down the road in a late 60s, jacked-up, muscle car—every chorus takes you up another gear and slams you further into your seat.

Ruth Ellsworth & Bill Carter

Stevie Ray Vaughan immortalized the hit song *Crossfire*, which was co-written by Ruth Ellsworth and Bill Carter. The husband and wife team have been writing songs together for more than ten years, and have seen their names listed in the credits of albums by more than thirty major recording artists. The couple also owns and operates the Eastside Cafe, unique for its vegetarian-style cuisine prepared straight from the organic herb and vegetable garden just out the door. When Ruth isn't writing songs, she's writing cookbooks. *Inside the Eastside* and *Soup Yourself*, two of Austin's most popular cookbooks, feature some of the favorite recipes she has created and served at the restaurant.

Inside the Eastside Tomato Basil Soup

Bill and Ruth have an herb and vegetable garden, and enjoy this recipe when fresh basil is plentiful and tomatoes are bursting forth from their garden.

- 2 tablespoons olive oil or butter
- ½ cup minced onion
- 1 teaspoon minced garlic
- 8 cups diced fresh tomatoes
- 2 teaspoons minced fresh basil
- 1 cup whipping cream (or half & half, or milk)
- salt and pepper to taste

In a medium saucepan, heat the olive oil or butter over medium heat. Add the onion and garlic, and sauté until soft, about 5–7 minutes. Remove from heat and set aside to cool.

When the onion mixture is cool, transfer it to a food processor or blender. Add 6 cups of the diced fresh tomatoes and the basil, and purée until smooth. Pour the puréed mixture into a large soup pot. Stir in the remaining 2 cups diced tomatoes, whipping cream, and salt and pepper. Stir well, and simmer over low heat for 25 minutes. Serve immediately. The soup may also be served chilled. Serves 2–4

Joe Ely

Gypsy Cowboy Posole

The main ingredient of posole, hominy, is slightly sweet and made from coarsely ground corn kernels. Joe says the posole is even tastier the second day.

2–2½	pounds pork roast, chicken, or pork chops
8	cups water
3	tablespoons chicken or vegetable bouillon
1	28-ounce can peeled tomatoes (do not drain)
2	15-ounce cans white hominy, drained
2	15-ounce cans yellow hominy, drained
3–4	roasted green chiles, peeled
1	tablespoon dried oregano
2	teaspoons red chile powder, preferably from Chimayo, New Mexico
2	teaspoons cumin
2	teaspoons dried, crushed red chiles (do not grind into a powder)
4	large garlic cloves, minced

In a large stock pot, brown the meat on all sides over medium heat. Remove meat from pot, debone, and cut into 1-inch cubes. Add water and bouillon to the pot, stirring in the browned bits, and cook until the bouillon is dissolved. Add the meat, and the remaining ingredients. Simmer over low heat for about 2 hours. Add more water, as needed. Serves 8–10

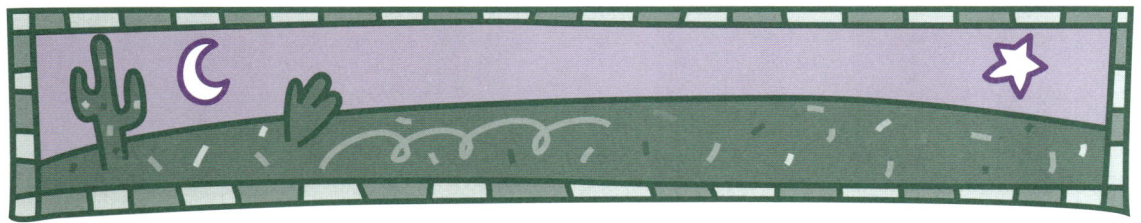

Michael Wilson

Everybody else romances the road. Joe Ely lives it. Call him what you will—wandering minstrel, gypsy cowboy, visionary poet or house rocker on fire—whatever he is, Joe has covered a lot of ground in his time. He has ridden the rails in a circus train, thumbed his way across the continent, and hopped boats destined for exotic lands—all in the relentless quest for the revelation that only a journey can satisfy. But for all the stamps on his passport, Joe Ely remains a Texas original. In Austin, where he now lives and works, a body of work that spans ten albums and his desire to put it all on the line each and every night have earned him status akin to royalty. His latest album, *Letter to Laredo*, demonstrates that the wanderer has found the revelation that satisfies fans and critics alike.

Michael Fracasso

Like his father and grandfather, Michael Fracasso worked in the steel mills of the Ohio River Valley. He still finds it hard to romanticize about "the dirt and the fire and the molten steel and the soot" of his youth. Fortunately, a steel worker's life was not to be his destiny. With the enthusiastic reception of CDs *love and trust* and *When I Lived In the Wild*, Michael has distinguished himself as one of Austin's finest singers and songwriters and a fast-rising national star. Indeed, music critic Dennis Constantine wrote that Michael's "songwriting is brilliant, and his music is steeped in American roots." Michael is married to Austin Parks Foundation executive director Paula Fracasso.

Insalata Pasta e Fagioli

I like to eat pasta all year long, but even I don't like to sit down to a hot bowl of spaghetti in the middle of the blistering Texas summer. So I've put together a version of Pasta e Fagioli served at room temperature and with a garden of fresh vegetables in mind. —Michael Fracasso

Beans:
- 1 pound dry small white beans
- 1 garlic clove, crushed
- ¼ cup fresh rosemary
- 1½ teaspoons salt

- ½ pound bowtie or wagon wheel pasta
- 1 clove garlic, crushed
- 1 bunch arugula, cleaned
- 1 head red romaine lettuce, cleaned
- 2 large ripe tomato, chopped
- ½ red bell pepper, chopped
- ½ cucumber, seeded and chopped
- ½ cup basil, chopped
- salt and pepper to taste
- ½ cup olive oil
- 3 tablespoons balsamic vinegar

To prepare beans: Place beans in large soup pot. Add water to cover by 2 inches. Add rosemary and salt. Slowly bring beans to boil, reduce heat and simmer for about 2½ hours. Allow to cool and drain. Reserve one cup of beans for this recipe, freeze remaining beans for later use.

Meanwhile, cook pasta according to directions on package. Drain and cool.

Rub crushed garlic around a very large salad bowl to season it. Fill salad bowl with lettuce and arugula, add tomato, pepper, cucumber, and basil.

Add the pasta, and 1 cup of the cooled and drained white beans. Season with salt and pepper. Blend olive oil and balsamic vinegar and pour over salad. Toss and serve. Serves 4–6

Fredericksburg Brewing Company

Jamaican Jerked Emu with Mango Chutney

Executive Chef Vickie Bonewitz is a master at cooking emu, and submits this recipe.

3-pound emu roast (or a pork boneless tenderloin, if emu is not available)

Mango chutney:
- 2 large mangoes, peeled and diced
- 2 teaspoons salt
- 1 fresh Scotch bonnet or habanero pepper
- 1 cup malt vinegar
- 4 teaspoons garlic, minced
- 2 tablespoons ginger, peeled and minced
- ¼ cup light brown sugar
- ½ cup raisins

Jerk spice:
- 4 teaspoons ground allspice
- 3 green onions, cut into 2-inch pieces
- 1 Scotch bonnet pepper or habenero pepper, quartered and seeded
- 4 teaspoons minced garlic
- 3 large sprigs fresh thyme, leaves only
- 1 whole bay leaf
- 4 teaspoons coarsely ground black pepper
- vegetable oil

To prepare chutney: Cover diced mangoes with salt, toss, and allow to sit for 30 minutes. Quarter and remove seeds from peppers and soak in malt vinegar for 15 minutes. Place vinegar and peppers in a heavy, medium saucepan along with garlic, ginger, and sugar. Simmer uncovered for 15 minutes. Add mangoes and raisins and simmer until thick and syrupy, about 30 minutes. May be made as much as 1–3 days ahead of time and stored in the refrigerator.

To prepare jerk spice: Place all the jerk spice ingredients, except the oil, in a food processor. Process until finely ground. Gradually add oil in a small stream until it has moistened spices enough to make a paste. Rub paste generously on emu or pork and allow to marinate for 12 hours, covered, in the refrigerator.

To roast emu: Preheat oven to 375°. Place the marinated emu on a roasting pan and sear for 15 minutes. Open oven, reducing heat to 300°. Close door, roast meat for 30 minutes more, or until a meat thermometer reads 130° for a moist, medium rare roast. We recommend a rare roast because emu's low fat content makes the meat tough and dry if cooked past medium. To roast the pork: Preheat oven to 350°. Place pork on a roasting pan, and cook for 40–50 minutes, or until a meat thermometer reads 150°–160°. To serve, carve meat in thin slices and spoon a dollop of chutney on each slice. Serves 6–8

Lynn A. Herrmann

Before opening the Fredericksburg Brewing Company, owners Dick Estenson, Laird Laurence, and John Davies visited regional breweries in Germany, Hungary, and the Czech Republic. They were researching brew pub decor and recipes for brews. As a result, the Fredericksburg Brewing Company is just how a good *gasthausbräuerei* should be. With fourteen foot tall ceilings made of hammered tin and a bar constructed from longleaf yellow pine that runs the length of the room, the brewery's atmosphere is low-key and traditional. And then there's the beer—quite probably the best ales and lagers brewed in the state.

Fredericksburg Herb Farm

Bill Varney's love for growing plants took root early. On his eighth birthday, he started Bill's Greenhouse, his own nursery. Twenty-eight years later, Bill put his energy and talent into creating the 14-acre Fredericksburg Herb Farm with its large processing plant, commercial greenhouse, tea house, and the Herb Haus Bed and Breakfast. Bill's wife, Sylvia, spends her time teaching cooking classes, editing a quarterly herb farm newsletter, and designing labels for the various farm products—from lotions, to popcorn seasonings, to herbal honeys. Together the Varneys wrote *Along the Garden Path*, a beautiful book of recipes, gardening tips, and folklore.

Rosemary and Orange Rum Cake with Glorious Glaze

Rosemary and Orange Rum Cake, the number one selling dessert at the herb farm, is delightfully aromatic and a surprise to the taste buds.

Cake:
- 1 package 2-layer yellow cake mix
- 1 small package vanilla instant pudding mix
- 1 tablespoon finely minced fresh rosemary
- grated zest of 1 orange
- ½ cup water
- ½ cup canola oil
- ½ cup light rum
- 4 extra-large eggs
- 1 cup chopped pecans
- long rosemary sprigs and pale blue pansies for garnish

Glaze:
- ½ cup unsalted butter
- 1 cup granulated sugar
- ¼ cup water
- ¼ cup light rum

Preheat oven to 325°.

To prepare the cake: Spray a bundt pan with non-stick cooking spray. In a food processor, combine the cake mix, pudding mix, rosemary and orange zest. Process until well mixed. Add the water, canola oil, light rum, and mix. Add the eggs, one at a time, mixing well after each addition. Fold in the pecans. Pour the batter into the prepared bundt pan and bake for 1 hour, or until a wooden toothpick inserted into the middle of the cake comes out clean.

Meanwhile, to prepare the glaze: In a medium-sized saucepan, bring the butter, sugar, water, and rum to a boil. Boil until the mixture reaches a soft-ball stage, or 235° on a candy thermometer. Remove from heat.

Before removing the cake from the pan, pour the glaze over. Allow the glaze to soak into the cake completely before removing the cake from the pan. Invert cake so that the glazed top is facing up. Garnish with the rosemary springs and pansies. Makes 1 cake

Kinky Friedman

The Kinkster's Chicken Piccata

Cleve Hattersley cooks up this classic whenever he is at Kinky's ranch in Kerrville. Cleve says it is especially good on a chilly evening, and is best served over saffron rice or fresh linguine.

4	boneless, skinless chicken breasts
	all-purpose flour
¼	cup olive oil
1	teaspoon black pepper
1	teaspoon salt
¼	cup milk
¼	cup chicken broth or water
¼	cup white wine (optional)
2	tablespoons shredded fresh basil
	juice from 1 lemon

Slice each chicken breast cross-wise into several thin strips. Dust the chicken in the flour, and coat evenly. In a deep sauté pan, heat the olive oil over medium-high. Sprinkle chicken with salt and pepper, and lightly brown both sides. Remove chicken from sauté pan.

Reduce the heat to medium, add the milk, chicken broth or water, white wine, fresh basil and freshly squeezed lemon juice. Simmer for 2–3 minutes until sauce is thickened. Stir in the chicken and coat evenly with the sauce. Lower the heat and simmer until the sauce is reduced, about 10–12 minutes. Do not overcook. Serve immediately. Serves 4

Kinky Friedman takes irreverence to new comedic heights. Some Kinkyisms: "The majority of my fans are either very smart or very dumb." Or, "I've always seen a lot of parallels between my life and Jesus Christ. We're both Jewish, we both didn't get married, we both travel around irritating people." *Texas Monthly* called him the "Jewish Will Rogers." And, *Newsday* called him the "Lenny Bruce of country." One thing for sure, whether he's wearing the Stetson of a singer and songwriter or the hat of a mystery novelist, Kinky isn't boring. Kinky lives in a lavishly appointed 14-foot trailer on his ranch in the Texas Hill Country near Kerrville.

Steven Fromholz

Steven Fromholz is a Texan by birth, an entertainer by compulsion, and a good cook by choice and practice. Born in Temple, Bell County, Texas, in 1945, this musical raconteur has spent the last thirty plus years playing and singing his original brand of music all across America and throughout the Lone Star state. Also an actor, playwright, and river guide, Steven takes great pride in his cooking—a gift his family and friends are grateful for.

Go Native Marinade

I made this one up whilst I was searching for a non-tomato based marinade-sauce for brisket and ribs. —Steven Fromholz

- 1 cup strong black coffee
- ½ cup black strap molasses
- ½ cup dark rum
- ½ cup butter
- ½ cup soy sauce
- 1 tablespoon salt
- 1 tablespoon cayenne pepper (mas o menos)
- Juice of two lemons

Mix all ingredients in a medium sauce pan. Bring to boil over medium heat, then lower heat, and simmer, uncovered, for 30 minutes. Refrigerate until ready to use.

This is a great marinade for beef cuts, such as brisket, ribs, or even flank steak; and wild game, such as venison and duck. Marinate meat overnight in the refrigerator or for several hours at room temperature. Then baste meat with remaining sauce while barbecuing making sure to thoroughly cook all marinade. Alternately, this can be used as a barbecue sauce for chicken and pork. Just brush it on in the last few minutes of grilling. Makes 3½ cups

Héctor Galán

Director Héctor Salsa

Héctor recommends serving his salsa in a nice imported Mexican bowl with tortilla chips. Add some Tejano music and cervezas, and you have a fiesta. Olé.

- 6 fresh jalapeño peppers, chopped
- 3 medium tomatoes, chopped
- 2–4 tablespoons tomato sauce
- 2 tablespoons onion powder
- 2 tablespoons garlic powder
- salt and pepper to taste

In a medium saucepan, place the jalapeño peppers and tomatoes, and bring to a boil. Lightly mash the tomatoes with a fork. Allow to boil for 5 minutes. Drain the liquid off. Put the jalapeño peppers and tomatoes in a food processor or blender. Add the tomato sauce. The amount of tomato sauce you add depends upon how hot you like your salsa: add more tomato sauce for a milder salsa. Blend well. Add the onion powder, garlic powder, and salt and pepper, and continue to blend. Makes about 2½–3 cups

Don Bentz

The fact that Héctor Galán was born in 1953 in San Angelo and came of age during the Chicano civil-rights movement of the 1960s resonates in nearly every documentary film he produces from his West Austin office. His most recent documentary, *Chicano! History of the Mexican-Civil Rights Movement* aired on PBS, and chronicled the Vietnam anti-war movement, the life of Cesar Chavez and his work with the United Farm Workers, and other topics. The cultural richness of Tejano music was celebrated in his *Songs of the Heartland*, winner of the 1995 Special Jury Award at CineFestival. Héctor explains that his documentaries inspect "that no-man's-land, from the border north, where you're neither Mexican nor American."

Jimmie Dale Gilmore

Caroline Greyshock 1996

The wide-open nothingness of West Texas breeds two kinds of kids: ones who won't see past the horizon, and those who see a horizon of promises beckoning them. Amarillo native Jimmie Dale Gilmore obviously looked at the horizon from the latter point of view. Music, Jimmie concluded, was a ticket to ride. And he's ridden it across the state into Austin, where he unleashed his latest albums, *Spinning Around the Sun* and *Braver, Newer World*, to the world's gratification. After the release of *Spinning*, Jimmie found himself launched into a series of high-profile situations: dueting with 10,000 Maniacs for the edification of Jay Leno and the *Tonight Show* audience and posing for a fashion layout in *Esquire* magazine. For Jimmie, the horizon looks wide open from Austin.

Janet's Spinach Enchiladas

My wife, Janet, makes these enchiladas and they really are my favorite. —Jimmie Dale Gilmore

Filling:
- 1–2 tablespoons olive oil
- 1 onion, chopped
- 3–4 garlic cloves, minced
- ¾ teaspoon ground cumin
- 2–4 poblano peppers, roasted, peeled, seeded, and chopped
- 2 pounds fresh spinach, washed, drained, chopped, and steamed (or 1 pound frozen spinach)
- 1 16-ounce package tofu or 1 pound cottage cheese
- 1½ cups grated Monterey Jack cheese, divided
- 1 cup of the following cooked vegetables or a combination: corn, artichoke hearts, pinto beans, black beans, squash, bell pepper

Sauce:
- 1 tablespoon olive oil
- 1 teaspoon cumin
- 1 tablespoon chili powder, or more to taste
- 1 16-ounce can tomatoes or tomato sauce
- 8 ounces sour cream, optional

- 1 dozen corn tortillas
- oil for frying

To prepare the filling: Heat the olive oil in a large skillet. Add the onion and garlic, and sauté until the onions are soft, about 5–7 minutes. Add the cumin and sauté for 1 more minute. In a large bowl, combine the onion-garlic mixture with the poblano peppers, spinach, tofu or cottage cheese, ¾ cup Monterey Jack cheese (reserve ¾ cup as topping), and the cooked vegetables.

To prepare the sauce: Heat the olive oil in a skillet and brown the cumin and chili powder over low heat, about 1 minute. Add the tomatoes or tomato sauce and the sour cream, if desired. Simmer for 10 minutes.

To prepare the enchiladas: Preheat oven to 375°. Soften the tortillas by frying them in hot olive oil for 15–30 seconds per side. They should be soft, but not crisp. Drain the oil from the tortillas on a paper towel. Place the tortillas, one at a time, on a flat surface. Spoon 2 spoonfuls of filling down the center of each tortilla and roll up. Place tortillas in an oiled 13x9-inch baking dish, seam side down. Pour the sauce over the tortillas, and top with the reserved cheese. Bake about 25 minutes, or until the cheese is bubbly. Serves 4–6.

Laura Groppe

A Girl's German Potato Salad

This recipe is from my grandmother who grew up in West Texas, near Waco. Yum, yum... sehr gut!! —Laura Groppe

- 2 pounds new potatoes, cleaned
- 4 bacon strips
- 1 medium white onion, chopped
- 2 tablespoons apple cider vinegar, or more to taste
- salt and pepper to taste

Boil potatoes in their skins in salted water in large covered pot until potatoes are just tender, about 15–20 minutes, depending upon their size. Let potatoes cool and peel them. Cut the potatoes in ¼-inch thick slices into a large salad bowl.

Meanwhile, fry bacon in heavy skillet until very crispy, but not burnt. Leave bacon in the skillet and add onion to the hot grease. Cooking onion slightly, about 1 minute. Let the onions cool slightly, and add vinegar, and salt and pepper. While still hot, pour onion mixture over potatoes. Toss and serve immediately. Serves 6

Laura Groppe thinks that young women are being left behind when it comes to virtual entertainment. A vast majority of computer games are targeted to males. And, many are violent or strictly academic products. But Laura hopes this will change, beginning with *Let's Talk About ME!* The CD-ROM series, developed by Laura's company Girl Games, is one of the first to address young women and their interests, including audio-video profiles of successful working women, and subjects like parents, sports, and fashion. Laura is well qualified to develop a model for young women. In the past, the Sweet Briar College graduate co-produced an Oscar-winning short film, *Session Man*, and music videos for groups like R.E.M. She even taught aerobics in Japan.

Kelly Gruber

La Zona Rosa's Pasta Gruber

Kurt Eller of La Zona Rosa submits this recipe on behalf of Kelly Gruber.

Texas native and former Toronto Blue Jays third baseman Kelly Gruber was twice named Canada's Favorite Athlete—a title usually reserved for that country's hockey heroes. Now, Canada's favorite athlete wants to turn La Zona Rosa into Austin's favorite restaurant. After an unbelievably successful baseball career—he was once the highest paid third baseman in the history of the game and has a World Series and a Golden Glove award under his belt—Kelly moved home to the Westbank in Austin. One of his greatest challenges these days is getting Austinites to flock to La Zona Rosa like they once flocked to the Toronto Blue Jay's stadium. Kelly is also busy raising four children, Samantha, Kody, Kassie, and Kyle with wife Tosca.

- 7 garlic cloves, roasted and chopped
- 3 inches fresh ginger root, peeled and finely chopped
- ¼ cup chopped fresh cilantro
- ½ cup sun-dried tomatoes, reconstituted and chopped
- ¾ cup grated Parmesan cheese
- ½ cup pine nuts, toasted
- 3 tablespoons olive oil
- 1 teaspoon freshly squeezed lime juice
- ½ teaspoon salt
- ¼ teaspoon black pepper
- 2 pounds penne pasta (You may substitute another pasta or try a flavored pasta, such as red chile penne.)
- 1 quart heavy cream
- ½ cup olive oil
- 2 chipotle chile peppers in adobo sauce, puréed
- 5 medium zucchini, cut into julienne
- ½ pound crawfish tail meat (Fresh is best, but frozen may be used in the off-season.)
- 1 teaspoon salt
- 8 ounces goat cheese, at room temperature
- 8 sprigs fresh cilantro

Place the garlic, ginger, cilantro, sun-dried tomatoes, Parmesan cheese, pine nuts, olive oil, fresh lime juice, and salt and pepper in a food processor. Purée until smooth. Set aside.

Bring a large pot of water to a boil, and cook the pasta according to the instructions on the package. Drain.

Meanwhile, pour the heavy cream into a large saucepan, and heat over medium for 10–15 minutes or until reduced by a third. Add the puréed sun-dried tomato-pine nut mixture to the cream. Stir in and simmer for 5 minutes. Add the pasta to the sauce and toss until it is coated evenly with the sauce. Keep warm.

In a skillet, heat the olive oil and puréed chipotle chiles. Add the julienned zucchini and crawfish tail meat, and sauté until meat is just cooked through, about 3–4 minutes. Stir in salt.

Spoon the pasta into 8 pasta bowls, and top with the zucchini and crawfish. Spoon a dollop of goat cheese over the pasta, and garnish with cilantro sprigs. Serves 8

Cliff Gustafson

Coach Gus' Swedish Pancakes

The batter for Swedish Pancakes is very thin—the pancake should be no more than a quarter-inch thick. You may have to add more milk to adjust the consistency.

- 1 egg
- 3 cups milk
- 2 cups all-purpose flour
- 1 teaspoon salt
- 1 teaspoon baking powder
- 2 tablespoons sugar
- 1 teaspoon vegetable oil for each batch of pancakes

In a large mixing bowl, beat the egg. Add the milk, and mix well. Stir in the flour, salt, baking powder, and sugar, and beat until smooth. Add more milk if necessary.

Heat a griddle over medium-high heat. Add the vegetable oil and coat the griddle. Spoon the pancake batter onto the griddle by heaping tablespoons. Cook until the bottoms are golden, the edges are just crispy, and bubbles begin to appear on the surface, about 1–1½ minutes. Flip, and cook for an additional 1 minute. Repeat, adding more vegetable oil to the griddle, as needed. Serve with butter and maple syrup. Makes about 20 pancakes

Since Darrell Royal hired coach Cliff "Gus" Gustafson in 1968, the Longhorn baseball team has won two national championships and twenty-one Southwest Conference regular-season titles. The team has participated in twenty-six NCAA Playoffs and seventeen College World Series. Coach Gus is the winningest coach in the history of NCAA Division I baseball. Well over 100 of his players have gone into professional baseball, and even more, inspired by Cliff's emphasis on academics, have turned to the law, medicine, and business. With a record like that, it's hard to believe the coach could have a life outside of baseball. But, Cliff and his wife, Janie, have raised three children, all of whom live in the Austin area. He spends his spare time golfing and playing with his grandchildren.

David Halley

Poetic Potato Leek Soup

Leeks, potatoes, and dill weed have an affinity for one another, as this soup attests. You might like to try Doyle Bramhall's healthy, homemade chicken broth for this recipe.

4	pounds potatoes, peeled and cut into ½-inch cubes
10	cups homemade chicken broth
6	tablespoons all-purpose flour
4	leeks (white and tender green), rinsed and chopped
10	tablespoons chopped fresh dill or 5 tablespoons dried dill weed, divided
2	cups chopped, cooked ham, or 2 cups cooked, shelled, and deveined shrimp
1½	cups heavy cream, or half & half
	salt to taste

Fill a large vegetable steamer with 2–3 inches of water, and steam the potatoes until they fall apart, about 30–35 minutes.

In a small bowl, stir ½ cup chicken broth into the flour. Whisk until smooth.

Meanwhile, in a large stock pot, combine the remaining chicken broth, flour-chicken broth mixture, leeks, and ½ of the dill weed. Cook at a rolling boil for 15 minutes. Add the steamed potatoes to the broth, lower heat, and simmer for 15–20 minutes. Stir in the ham or shrimp and remaining dill weed, and simmer for 5 more minutes.

Ladle the soup into a blender or food processor, and purée until smooth. Pour the puréed soup back into the stock pot. Stir in the cream and salt, and just heat through. Serve immediately. Serves 10–12

Singer and songwriter David Halley has always had strong regional acceptance. From his high school days playing a Sears Silvertone guitar at mixers and pool parties in Lubbuck, to more ambitious days in Austin, music critics have long anticipated broader national recognition and appreciation for his style. That appreciation crystallized with the release of his two albums, *Stray Dog Talk* and *Broken Spell*, and the top-ten country hit *Hard Livin'*, recorded by the late Keith Whitley. David, once dubbed "every man's street poet," is married to Susan Caldwell Halley, associate producer of *Austin City Limits*.

Thomas "Hollywood" Henderson

Hollywood's Chili Beans

Pinto beans are an important addition to any Tex-Mex meal. Their earthy flavor is enhanced in this recipe with the addition of turkey and a touch of sugar. And a blistering kick is derived from the large dose of chili powder and red pepper. This large batch is enough to feed a hungry football team.

- 3 pounds dried pinto beans, rinsed
- 2 bell peppers, chopped
- 2 whole onions, outer skins removed
- 4 tablespoons sugar
- 5 tablespoons chili powder
- 1 tablespoon crushed red pepper
- ½ tablespoon black pepper
- salt to taste
- 3 pounds ground turkey

Place the beans, bell peppers, and onion in a large stock pot. Cover with water by 2 inches. Boil, reduce heat, and simmer until the onions fall apart, about 1 hour. Add the sugar, chili powder, red pepper, black pepper and salt, and cook until the beans are nearly done, about 1 more hour. You may need to replenish the water from time to time. Crumble the ground turkey into the beans and mix well. Continue to simmer for 1 more hour. Serves 18–20

Jeff Cannon 1993

Few athletes have been as candid about their private lives as Thomas "Hollywood" Henderson. Thomas hustled to become one the of the best linebackers in NFL history when he played for the Dallas Cowboys. He then traveled from Super Bowl to cell block in a downward spiral that left him stripped of his career, family, and friends. The first NFL player to go public with his cocaine addiction, Thomas wrote of his flamboyant obsession with booze and drugs in the best-selling book *Out of Control*. Clean and sober since November 8, 1983, he travels from his home in Austin to schools, corporate meetings, and prisons around the world openly telling his story and encouraging kids to stay off drugs.

Hill Country Fruit Council

The Texas Hill Country is famous throughout Texas and the nation for producing some of the best tasting peaches in the country. The Hill Country Fruit Council is an association of the major Gillespie County peach growers, whose orchards are scattered throughout the fertile, sandy loam soil adjacent to the Pedernales River and its tributaries. Over thirty different varieties of peaches are grown in the area. Many growers have roadside stands or allow pick-your-own customers in their orchards. Biting into a tree-ripened Hill Country peach is one of life's simplest and most succulent pleasures.

Grandma's Chilled Peach Pie

5	fresh medium-sized Hill Country peaches
1	tablespoon lemon juice
½	cup sliced almonds, toasted
1	9-inch pie shell, baked
8	ounces cream cheese
2	tablespoons milk
1	teaspoon almond extract
1	tablespoon cornstarch
¼	cup sugar
1	tablespoon butter or margarine

Blanch peaches and peel. Cut into thin slices and place in bowl. Pour lemon juice over them and refrigerate.

Spread almonds in pie shell. In a medium mixing bowl, whip cream cheese, milk, and almond extract until light and creamy.

Pour cream cheese mixture over almonds and chill.

Arrange peach slices on pie filling, reserving peach juice. Combine cornstarch, and reserved peach juice and enough water to make ⅔ cup liquid. In small saucepan, combine cornstarch/peach juice mixture, sugar, and butter. Cook over medium heat, stirring frequently until clear and thickened. Let cool and pour over pie. Refrigerate and serve. Makes 1 pie

Tish Hinojosa

Traditional Ancho Sauce

The ancho chile is deep red-black, wrinkled, and semidry. It's also plump, flat, and ovalish in shape. It is not the long, skinny, dry red one—that's another chile. Because these chiles can vary in taste and picoso-ness (heat), you may have to experiment a bit. However, once the balance is right, you'll have an incomparably rich sauce for use in everything from enchiladas to posole, to menudo, or even "Texas Chili." My sauce is low in calories, too. **Provecho!** *—Tish Hinojosa*

2–3	handfuls ancho chiles
1–2	15-ounce cans tomato sauce, depending upon taste
	garlic cloves, minced, to taste
	comino (cumin), to taste
	salt to taste

Rinse the chiles. Fill the sink with water and let the chiles soak for 1 hour. Drain sink. Remove the stems and seeds from the chiles. Place the chiles in a large pot of water. Heat to a boil, and cook on high for 5–10 minutes. Lower heat and simmer for another 30 minutes.

Bring the pot of chiles to the counter where a blender is sitting. Also have a medium pot, sieve and big spoon on hand. Spoon the chiles with some of the chile juice or water into the blender a few spoonfuls at a time, and purée. Make sure there is enough chile juice to blend. Too much juice, and the sauce will be too soupy. Too little, and the sauce will not blend.

Arrange a sieve over the medium pot. Pour the puréed chile mixture through the sieve, using a spoon to push the solids through. This sieving process can be achieved by whatever means you have. I use a big hand-held sieve and a large spoon. What drops into the pot is creamy, rich, pure chile. What stays in the sieve is skin and left-over seeds.

In a large saucepan, combine the chiles with the tomato sauce, garlic, comino, and salt. Simmer over medium-low heat until thickened. Experiment for the perfect blend of garlic and comino. The tomato sauce will curb bitterness, if any. Be careful, though, as it may taste too tomato-ey. You may add some of the chile juice if the sauce is too thick.

Wyatt McSpadden

Tish Hinojosa's voice breaks down the boundaries that sometimes form between the Latino and Anglo cultures. On her latest record, *Dreaming from the Labyrinth/Soñar del Laberinto*, she saunters easily between Spanish and English in songs that connect her heritage as a child of Mexican immigrants with the dreamlike process of making music in her native Texas. Tish grew up in San Antonio and recalls, "My mother listened to Mexican radio in the kitchen, and she loved the finer, romantic side of Mexican culture. My dad loved the fun accordion music and *conjunto* tunes of the juke box. Of course, through my older sisters, I was immersed in the jangly pop of the sixties, the Byrds, and the Beatles." So, it's no accident that the celebrated Austin singer-songwriter who moves so easily between languages, also moves gracefully between genres. *Labyrinth* captures the essence of pop, rock, and folk.

Champ Hood

Champ Hood has charmed audiences all over the world with his genteel Southern stage presence and dynamic instrumental work on the acoustic guitar and fiddle. And he charms audiences at Threadgill's restaurant on Wednesday nights as host and band leader of the supper sessions that often turn into impromptu jams with an array of Austin's finest musicians. The Texas Music Hall of Famer's elegant guitar work can be heard on Lyle Lovett's Grammy award-winning album, *Lyle Lovett and His Large Band*, and Champ's raucous fiddle playing and vocals can be found on albums by Austin friends Toni Price, Jerry Jeff Walker, and David Halley. Champ has lived in Austin since the mid 1970s, when he moved there with the legendary folk trio Uncle Walt's Band.

River City Green Bean Rolls

I really don't do that much cooking, but I do enjoy that "manly" thing of firing up the grill and trying to create some good BBQ. This is one of my favorite side dishes. —Champ Hood

- 1 pound fresh green beans, rinsed
- 8 slices bacon
- 1 tablespoon fresh rosemary, crushed
  salt and freshly ground pepper to taste

Prepare the coals for grilling.

Trim the ends from the green beans. Bring a large pot of water to a boil, and add the beans. Simmer until the beans are just tender, about 3–4 minutes. Drain.

On a flat surface, place 2 slices of bacon side-by-side, with the long edges overlapping. Place a fourth of the green beans at one end of the bacon slices. Sprinkle the beans with rosemary and salt and pepper. Roll the beans up in the bacon. Wrap each roll in aluminum foil, creating a tight seal.

Repeat until you have 4 bundles. Place the bundles on the grill or directly in the mesquite coals. Cook for 15 minutes, turning often, until the bacon is just crisp. Serves 4

Tobe Hooper

Texas Chainsaw Chili

As for the story behind this recipe, if you saw Texas Chainsaw Massacre, *you'll know where I got the idea for my Chainsaw Chili. Leatherface, did, however, use some other "ingredients" that aren't included in my personal version. —Tobe Hooper*

- 4 pounds coarsely ground beef
- 2 large onions, coarsely chopped
- 5 garlic cloves, finely chopped
- 1 cup chopped celery
- 1 cup sliced mushrooms
- 2 tablespoons crushed dried red peppers
- 5 tablespoons mild red chili powder
- 3 tablespoons ground cumin
- 3 cups water
- 2 15-ounce cans tomato sauce
- 2 28-ounce cans chopped, peeled tomatoes
- 2 16-ounce cans pinto beans, drained
  grated sharp Cheddar cheese and freshly chopped onions for garnish

In a large stock pot, cook the meat, onion, garlic, celery, and mushrooms over medium heat until the meat is no longer pink, about 5–7 minutes. Stir in the crushed red chile peppers, chili powder, cumin, water, tomato sauce, tomatoes, and pinto beans. Bring to a boil. Lower heat, and simmer, uncovered, for 1–2 hours. Stir often, and adjust the seasonings according to your taste. If too thick, add water and masa harina or flour to thicken. Serve topped with cheese and onions. Serves 10–12

Before you get the idea the director of *Texas Chainsaw Massacre*, Austin-native Tobe Hooper, is as brutally deranged and disturbing as the movie, you should know that the story was inspired by real-life cannibal Edward Gein. Tobe, truly a genuinely nice guy, merely brought the creation to the big screen—and forever changed the meaning of the word "power tool." The film has been inducted into the Horror Hall of Fame and is in the permanent collection of the New York Museum of Modern Art. Tobe's most ambitious and commercial movie was the phenomenally successful *Poltergeist*. Tobe now presides over his own film company, Amazon Films, in association with the Walt Disney Company in Santa Monica, California.

Kay Bailey Hutchison

The seat that Kay Bailey Hutchison occupies holds special significance for the freshman Senator. Kay is the great-great granddaughter of Charles S. Taylor, who signed the Texas Declaration of Independence and was a friend of and law partner of Thomas Jefferson Rusk, the first Texan to serve in the U.S. Senate. Today, Kay sits in Rusk's seat. A graduate of the University of Texas law school and the first woman to represent her state in the U.S. Senate, Kay was elected by the largest margin of votes ever received in the country against a sitting, incumbent senator. Kay is married to Ray Hutchison, a former colleague from the Texas House. They fund two scholarships at the University of Texas.

Shadywood Showdown Chili

Did I discover the key to world peace? Judging from the attention I received, one might have thought so. But no, it was a chili contest that garnered all that attention — and I won! I recaptured for Texas the coveted Congressional Club Chili Cook-Off championship.

Of course, every triumph brings controversy in its wake. Since the Associated Press transmitted the prize-winning chili recipe across its wire, I have been the target of numerous attacks.

As you might guess, most of the criticism aimed at the chili which I submitted focused on our use of one highly controversial ingredient. If you're a native Texan, you would immediately say... of course... beans! I have long been aware of the vast chasm stretching across Texas which separates the pro-beans-in-the-chili advocates from the anti-beans-in-the-chili purists. It is closely akin to the long-standing rivalry between Longhorn and Aggie fans.

I am also aware that nothing I say, nor the most ambrosial recipe which can be imagined, will move members of either faction one iota. On this subject, minds are sealed at an early age.

But there were other points of criticism aimed at our chili recipe, as well. Several commentators objected to the use of kidney beans rather than pinto beans. This was actually based on necessity, bean selection here in Washington being limited.

(Just to illustrate the cultural differences inherent in such a contest, I point with horror to the submission by a member of Congress who shall be nameless. His recipe included pasta—yes, that's right, pasta, as in macaroni. Surely such a bizarre ingredient eclipses the bean debate entirely.)

Houston columnist Leon Hale, whom I otherwise have always admired, took issue with the inclusion of green peppers. I admit this is borderline. But surely it's an exaggeration to assert, as he did, that such ingredients add up to a "recipe for disaster."

Regardless of such debate, I am proud to have represented my state so successfully and to have returned the trophy to its rightful place: in the office of a U.S. Senator from Texas. It has been won by member of Congress from other states for five years—now that is a scandal!

But I will let you be the judge. My staff leader in this project, Natasha Moore, and I submit it to you for a vote. This is our story and we're stickin' to it!
—Kay Bailey Hutchison

2	tablespoons olive oil, divided
2	medium yellow onions, diced, divided
2	green peppers, diced, divided
	salt, pepper, and garlic powder to taste
2½	pounds ground sirloin
4	tablespoons mole sauce, divided
2	8-ounce cans tomato sauce
4	tablespoons chili powder mix
1	16-ounce can kidney beans, drained (optional)

In a medium-sized sauté pan, heat 1 tablespoon olive oil. Sauté half the onion and pepper until the onion is soft, about 5 minutes. Stir in the salt and pepper, and garlic powder. In a separate skillet, brown the meat over medium-heat, leaving the meat in chunks. Drain off the fat. Add the onion-pepper mixture to the meat. Stir in 3 tablespoons mole sauce. Transfer the meat mixture to a large stock pot. Add the tomato sauce along with 2 or 3 cans of water. Stir in 3 tablespoons chili powder mix. Bring to a boil. Add remaining mole sauce, and simmer for 1 hour. Stir occasionally. Meanwhile, sauté the remaining onion and pepper in 1 tablespoon olive oil until onion is soft. Add to the stock pot, along with the kidney beans. Add the remaining 1 tablespoon chili powder, and cook for an additional 15 minutes. Serve with your favorite fixins. Serves 4–6

The Instruments

The Instruments bring about their distinctive sound with modest tools—a bunch of strings, a set of drums and weathered notebooks full of witty, gritty American poetry. Indeed, vocalist David Woody's honest lyrics have been compared to Woody Guthrie and Bob Dylan, and the band's unique blend of punk, rock, folk and country to the Ramones and Elvis Costello. Their gun-slinging guitar style tempered with a pioneer optimism has endured since 1983, and the release of their fifth album, *Speed of Sound*, is a favorite among Austin's alternative-music lovers. The Instruments is comprised of David, Clay Daniel, Ron Marks, and Steve Chapman.

Brownies for Lazy, Decadent People

As the saying goes, the best things in life are free, but they definitely aren't fat-free.

- 1 cup butter
- 1 cup granulated sugar
- 1 cup dark brown sugar, packed
- ¾ cup cocoa
- 3 eggs
- 2 teaspoons vanilla extract
- 1 cup all-purpose flour
- 2 teaspoons baking powder
- 1 cup chopped pecans or chopped walnuts

Preheat oven to 350°.

Lightly grease a 13x9-inch pan. In a large saucepan, melt the butter over low heat. Stir in the granulated sugar, brown sugar, and cocoa and whisk until the sugars have dissolved and the mixture is smooth. Do not let the mixture boil. Remove from heat, and set aside to cool for 2 minutes. Add the eggs, one at a time, mixing thoroughly. Stir in the vanilla. In a mixing bowl, mix the flour and baking powder together. Gradually add the flour to the cocoa mixture. Fold in the pecans or walnuts. Pour the brownie batter into the prepared pan, and bake for 30 minutes. Cool before cutting into squares. Makes about 1 dozen 2½-inch brownies

Molly Ivins

Hungarian Paprika Mushrooms

Paprika sprinkled on a dish as a garnish really doesn't do justice to the great flavor of paprika from Hungary. To get the full flavor of the spice, use several teaspoons and be sure to cook it a few minutes, just as curry powder needs to be cooked to develop its true flavor. Hungarian paprika is the world's finest. Paprika harvests are graded for quality like wine vintages—with good and better years! Sweet paprika really just means less hot. —Molly Ivins

- 2 tablespoons unsalted sweet butter
- 2 tablespoons finely minced shallot, or green onion
- 3/4 pound mushrooms, washed, trimmed, stem left on, slice into quarters
- 1/2 teaspoon Kosher salt
- 1/4 teaspoon freshly ground black pepper
- 2 teaspoons finely chopped fresh marjoram, or 1/2 teaspoon dried marjoram
- 2 teaspoons hot or sweet Hungarian paprika, or 1 teaspoon of each
- 1/4 teaspoon all-purpose flour (Don't be tempted to use more.)
- 1/3 cup light sour cream, or crème fraîche

In a large skillet, melt the butter. Add the shallot or onion, and mushrooms and sauté over medium heat for 5 minutes, stirring occasionally. Lower the heat. In a small mixing bowl, combine the salt and pepper, marjoram, paprika, and flour, and mix together well. Stir the paprika mixture into the mushrooms and sauté for an additional 2–3 minutes to develop the flavor of the paprika. Just before serving, stir in the sour cream or crème fraîche and heat through. Do not boil. Serves 4

Tomas Pantin

Armed with degrees from Smith College and Columbia University, a young Molly Ivins attacked the untamed newspaper world like a wild bull. Her gusto landed her her first job at the *Houston Chronicle* in the Complaint Department, but she rapidly rose to become sewer editor. After a succession of muck-raking jobs, she eventually joined the staff of the *New York Times*, where as Rocky Mountain Bureau Chief, she covered nine mountain states and was often tired. Experiencing a masochistic streak in 1982, Molly returned once again to her home state of Texas, where she has been a political columnist ever since. The Austin resident and three-time finalist for the Pulitzer Prize says her two greatest honors include having the Minneapolis police force name its mascot pig after her and once being banned from Texas A&M.

Johnny Dee and the Rocket 88s

White Scratch Cake with Texas Pecan Icing

The following recipe is so scrumptious that it is addicting. It was passed down from the last century to my mom, Kathleen Landers, who is a master baker. She can trace it back more than five generations. —Johnny Dee

For the past 20 years, this zany and nostalgic band has offered a 1950s version of rock and roll complete with the haircut, the look, and the attitude. Johnny Dee and the Rocket 88s—Johnny Dee, T-Bone Keltone, Little Dickie Lee Dickins, Jimmy Nitro, and Mike Technique—have performed their unique brand of fast-paced medleys for millions of people. They have appeared on national television, and with such artists as Dick Clark, Wolfman Jack, James Brown, and Tanya Tucker. They have performed for presidents, international royalty, the Dallas Cowboys, Bob Hope and many others. Their award-winning music video, *Don't Mess with Texas*, which railed against litter, has been acclaimed as one of the most effective public service campaigns in the history of advertising.

Cake:
- 2 cups granulated sugar
- 2/3 cup shortening
- 4 eggs
- 2 cups all-purpose flour
- 2 teaspoons baking powder
- 1/4 teaspoon salt
- 1 cup milk (2% or whole)
- 2 1/2 tablespoons vanilla

Icing:
- 1 1/4 cups granulated sugar
- 1 cup milk
- 1/4 cup butter or margarine
- 2 cups ground pecans
- 1 teaspoon vanilla

Preheat oven to 350°. Lightly grease three 9-inch, or four 8-inch round cake pans.

To prepare the cake: In a medium bowl, cream sugar and shortening at low speed with mixer. Increasing speed to medium, add eggs, one at a time, beating well after each addition, until all eggs are added and mixture is smooth.

In a large bowl, sift the flour with the baking powder and salt. Add egg mixture alternately with milk to flour mixture, beating at medium speed until all ingredients are moist. Stir in vanilla.

Pour cake batter into prepared pans and bake for 20 minutes. Cakes should be lightly browned and spring back from a light pressure in the center. Cool pans on wire rack for 10 minutes. Loosen cakes and turn out on a smooth cloth.

To prepare icing: In a medium saucepan, bring the sugar, milk and butter or margarine to a boil. Turn down heat, and stir in pecans gradually, until mixture thickens. Remove from heat and stir in vanilla. Continue to stir until mixture has cooled. Spread on cake. *(This icing is great on ice cream, too!)* Makes 1 cake

Eric Johnson

Roasted Red Bell Pepper Pesto

Pesto sauce over your favorite pasta is a quick solution for dinner after a busy day. It takes just minutes to prepare, and red bell peppers are packed with vitamins A, C, and E. Eric prefers capellini or farfalle pasta with his Roasted Red Bell Pepper Pesto.

- 5 large red bell peppers
- 6 garlic cloves
- ½ cup pine nuts, pecans, or walnuts
- ¼ cup olive oil
- 1 cup grated Parmesan cheese
- dash of salt and pepper
- 1 pound dry pasta, cooked according to the instructions

Preheat oven to 400°. Place the whole peppers on a cookie sheet, and roast for 20–25 minutes, until the meat is tender and the skin just begins to blacken. Allow to cool so that the peppers may be handled.

Increase the oven setting to broil. Cut the bell peppers in half lengthwise. Remove the seeds, stems, and ribs. Lay the peppers skin side up on a cookie sheet, and place directly below the elements and broil, until the skins of the peppers are charred or blackened and begin to blister. Remove peppers from the oven and place them in a covered bowl, or plastic or paper bag. Let the peppers steam for 15 minutes. Remove the peppers from the bowl or bag, and slip off the charred skins.

To a food processor, add the roasted bell peppers, garlic cloves, pine nuts, olive oil, Parmesan cheese, and salt and pepper. Purée until smooth. Store the pesto in a sealed jar in the refrigerator for up to 1 week.

Prepare your favorite pasta according to the instructions on the box. Drain. Dollop the pesto on the pasta, toss, and serve. Serves 4

Guitar virtuoso Eric Johnson is no stranger to music awards and critical acclaim. On his own turf, he has been honored repeatedly at the Austin Music Awards as Best Electric Guitarist and Best Acoustic Guitarist—no small honor from one of the world's most guitar-intensive cities. Nationally, he continues to garner accolades, beginning with his debut album *Tones*, which was nominated for a Grammy. For four years in a row *Guitar Player* magazine voted Eric the Best Overall Guitarist on the planet. His guitar style, which knows no boundaries, has been influenced by the other guitar great, B.B. King, with whom he toured for five exciting weeks. At home in Austin and always ready to dazzle the audience, Eric may exchange guitar licks with Jimmie Vaughan or jam with harp player Kim Wilson.

Lady Bird Johnson

Of the many titles—journalist, First Lady, Texan of the Year—Lady Bird Johnson has held in her accomplished life, the title she is most proud of is that of Environmentalist. Her ties to nature may have begun early in life when a nursemaid exclaimed she was "as purty as a lady bird," and the nickname stuck. During her White House years, Lady Bird was committed to America's beautification; the Highway Beautification Act of 1965 was the result of her influence. In Austin, she chaired the Town Lake Beautification Project, a community effort to create a nature trail along the Colorado River. On her 70th birthday, Lady Bird founded the National Wildflower Research Center, and donated 60 acres and a sum of money to the non-profit organization, which is dedicated to the preservation of native plants. Lady Bird continues to live at the LBJ Ranch in Stonewall and has a house in northwest Austin.

LBJ Ranch Spicy Cheddar Wafers

Cheese wafers are a ranch staple and are served for just about any occasion—with salads, with cocktails, or just when one of the grandchildren gets the munchies. —Lady Bird Johnson

- 1 cup butter or margarine, at room temperature
- 2 cups all-purpose flour
- 8 ounces sharp Cheddar cheese, grated
- 1 teaspoon cayenne pepper
- ½ teaspoon salt
- 2 cups Rice Krispies cereal

Preheat oven to 350°.

In a mixing bowl, cut the butter into the flour using a pastry blender. Add the cheese and seasonings and mix well. Fold in the Rice Krispies cereal.

Drop the cheese mixture by small rounds on an ungreased cookie sheet. Flatten with a spoon.

Bake for 15 minutes. Do not let the wafers get too brown. Makes 24 wafers

Milton Jung

Arresting Barbecued Pork Loin Chops

Sheriff Jung won the 1981 Texas Pork Cook-Off, and then the 1992 National Pork Cook-Off, held in Des Moines, Iowa, with this recipe.

6	16-ounce center cut pork loin chops, about 2 inches thick
	salt and freshly ground pepper
½	cup butter or margarine
½	cup tomato juice
½	cup ketchup
¼	cup tomato sauce
2½	tablespoons vinegar
1	tablespoon lemon juice
1	tablespoon mustard with horseradish
1	tablespoon hot sauce
1	tablespoon Worcestershire sauce
1	1½-ounce package quick instant chili mix
1	20-ounce can pineapple slices, drained

Season pork chops with salt and pepper. Cover and refrigerate for 1-2 hours.

Meanwhile, prepare coals and barbecue sauce. Melt butter in a medium saucepan. Add tomato juice, ketchup, tomato sauce, vinegar, lemon juice, mustard, hot sauce, Worcestershire sauce, and chili mix. Cook over medium heat stirring constantly, until well combined and heated through.

Place chops on grill approximately 6 inches above medium coals. Slow cook the chops for about 30 minutes. Turn and baste with sauce; cook an additional 30-45 minutes. Remove chops and place on a double sheet of heavy-duty aluminum foil. Top each with 1-2 pineapple slices and a small amount of sauce. Fold aluminum foil over chops and seal. Return to grill. Cover grill, if possible, and cook chops over low heat for 1 hour more. Serve with remaining sauce on the side. Serves 6

Milton Jung is the popular sheriff of the Texas Hill Country's Gillespie County. In fact, he is so popular that he was unopposed in the last election. A Fredericksburg native, Milton is easy-going, yet serious about his job, which includes overseeing nearly twenty officers. Although the Hill Country is becoming one of the most popular spots in the country to move to, it is still small enough that almost everyone knows everyone else, and keeping livestock off the road is still one of law enforcement's major preoccupations. Milton is also famous for his cooking, and whenever there is a department get-together he's in charge of the barbecue and the chili. Milton and his wife, Maxine, have two grown children.

Emily Kaitz

Larry J. Murphy

A musician since 1965, Emily Kaitz describes herself as an obscure and happy person. But her songs are well-known and many have been performed and recorded by a variety of artists. After hearing her song, *Gene Pool*, a critic for the *Ft. Worth Star Telegram* called it "one of the cleverest numbers ever performed by an earthling." Other songs have been as inspirational. Friends have been known to leave her tune *Middle-Aged Rock & Rollers Are So Damn Cute* on their answering machines for months on end. Emily's independent label, Pingleblobber, has produced six cassettes of her original work, and she has toured throughout Texas and the United States. A musician by night and a piano-tuner technician by day, Emily says, unlike other musicians, she has no intention of giving up her day job.

Dreaded Yuppie Sun-dried Tomato Pesto

Like basil pesto, this tomato pesto will quickly become a staple in a house where meals are needed posthaste and time is short. The first half of this recipe can be stored in the refrigerator or freezer for weeks. Before serving, simply, cook the bell pepper and add the rest of the ingredients. This recipe works well as a pizza topping also.

"Yes, I've turned into a dreaded yuppie in my middle age. I actually eat stuff like this." —Emily Kaitz

- 3 ounces (about 1 cup, slightly packed) sun-dried tomatoes
- 1 cup boiling water
- juice of ½ lemon
- ½ teaspoon lemon zest
- 4 garlic cloves
- ½ teaspoon red pepper flakes
- ¼ cup olive oil (extra virgin, if you can find it)
- 1-1½ pounds dry pasta
- 1 red bell pepper, diced
- 2 tablespoons olive oil
- ½ cup pitted black olives (Kalamata or Nicoise are best), chopped
- ½ cup pine nuts
- ½ cup Parmesan cheese, grated
- salt to taste

Pour boiling water over sun-dried tomatoes and let sit for 15 minutes. Pour off half of the water, reserving it for later.

In food processor, blend sun-dried tomatoes with water, lemon juice, lemon zest, garlic, red pepper flakes, and olive oil. Blend to a smooth consistency, adding reserved water if necessary. This portion of the recipe can be made in advance and stored in the freezer or refrigerator for use in the future.

Sauté red bell pepper in olive oil for 5 to 10 minutes over medium heat. While sautéing pepper, cook pasta following directions on package. In large bowl, mix pesto mixture (should be at room temperature), sautéed pepper, olives, pine nuts, and Parmesan cheese. Mix thoroughly.

Toss with cooked pasta. Serves 6

Beverly Kearney

Make Tracks Chicken

When you are in a big hurry and really need to make tracks, try this baked chicken recipe. It just takes a few minutes to throw together, and voilá, dinner is on the table. Beverly suggests serving it over rice.

- 6 boneless, skinless chicken breasts
- ¾ cup grated Swiss cheese
- 2 10¾-ounce cans cream of chicken soup
- 1 cup white wine
- ¾ cup bread crumbs
- butter

Preheat oven to 350°.

Place the chicken breasts in a 13x9-inch pan. Sprinkle the Swiss cheese over the chicken. In a mixing bowl, combine the soup and wine, and pour over the chicken. Sprinkle with bread crumbs and dot each breast with butter. Bake for 30–40 minutes. Serves 6

Before Beverly Kearney was a great track and field coach, she was a great athlete. She qualified for the U.S. Olympic trials in the 200 meter in 1980, and was selected as Athlete of the Year and MVP at Auburn University. Perhaps her winning record as a coach comes from her winning attitude as a student athlete. A relative newcomer to the University of Texas, Coach Kearney has guided the UT track and field team toward a league crown in every event since 1993. The versatile leader has coached All-Americans in the field events, sprints, and distance events, and she has coached students to Olympic medals and world records. Beverly wins respect from her peers as well as her fans—she was voted president of the Track and Field Coaches' Association, and in winning form, she is the first woman and first African-American to hold that position.

Robert Earl Keen

Robert Earl Keen's shows are almost always a sell-out, whether he is playing at the nation's largest music festival, Austin's South by Southwest, or the world's largest honky-tonk, Fort Worth's Billy Bob's Texas. His musical journey began as a kid when he hung out at Czech polka parties, and continued at Texas A&M where he was introduced to bluegrass and country by his friend Lyle Lovett. Leaving Texas A&M with a degree in English, the musical storyteller, whose style is perhaps best defined as "roadhouse rowdy," is now traveling the route from cult hero to national recording artist via a contract signed with Arista/Texas. Robert Earl lives with his wife, Kathleen, in Bandera.

Sonora Death Row Casserole

What follows is my wife Kathleen's adaptation of a popular dish in the San Antonio area. She renamed the dish after a Blackie Farrell song which I have sung for many years. Kathleen has made this dish many, many times for visiting fellow singer/songwriters and she served it during the recording of my fourth record, A Bigger Piece of Sky. *—Robert Earl Keen*

- 3 cups thinly-sliced zucchini, steamed or microwaved for 3–4 minutes
- 1 cup fresh corn kernels, steamed or microwaved for 3–4 minutes
- 2 cups tomato sauce
- 1 teaspoon apple cider vinegar
- 1 tablespoon chili powder
- ½ teaspoon cayenne pepper
- ½ teaspoon ground cumin
- 10 corn tortillas, quartered and fried
- 2 cups grated sharp Cheddar cheese
- 8 ounces Ortega chile peppers, chopped
- sour cream and chopped green onions for garnish

Preheat oven to 350°.

In a large mixing bowl, combine the zucchini, corn kernels, tomato sauce, and apple cider vinegar. In a small bowl, combine the chili powder, cayenne pepper, and cumin. Mix the spices in with the zucchini-corn mixture. Fold in the tortillas pieces and cheese. Pour into a large casserole, and bake for 30–45 minutes. Serve with sour cream and chopped green onions as garnish. Serves 4–6

Jimmy LaFave

Rave LaFave Veggie Chili

Chili doesn't have to include red meat to be hearty and warm the tummy. Here the pinto beans and bulgur add substance and are a healthy substitute for beef. Jimmy's recipe has an imposing list of spices and vegetables, but is really quite easy to make.

¼ teaspoon cayenne pepper	1 cup corn kernels
1½ tablespoons ground cumin	1 4-ounce can chopped green chiles
3 tablespoons chili powder	2 cups tomato juice
1 tablespoon dried oregano	2 fresh tomatoes, seeded and chopped
¼ cup olive oil	¼ cup fresh lemon juice
2 large onions, chopped	2 tablespoons Worcestershire sauce
3 garlic cloves, minced	½ cup white wine
¾ cup chopped celery	1 15-ounce can pinto beans, rinsed and drained
1 red bell pepper, cored, seeded, and chopped	½ cup bulgur wheat
1 yellow bell pepper, cored, seeded, and chopped	salt and pepper to taste
	½ bunch fresh basil, slivered
2 carrots, peeled and cut on the diagonal	sour cream and chopped scallions, for garnish

In a small bowl, combine the cayenne pepper, cumin, chili powder, and oregano. Set aside. In a large pot, heat the olive oil over medium heat. Add the onion and garlic, and sauté until the onion is just limp, about 4 minutes. Add the celery, red bell pepper, yellow bell pepper, carrots, corn, and green chiles. Sauté over medium-low heat for 10 minutes, stirring often. Add the tomato juice, fresh tomatoes, lemon juice, Worcestershire sauce, wine, pinto beans, bulgur wheat, and salt and pepper. Bring to a boil. Reduce heat, and simmer for 40 more minutes. Just before serving, stir in the basil and cook until just wilted. Serve with sour cream and chopped scallions on the side. If the chili is too thick, thin with tomato juice. Serves 8

Don't be deceived by Jimmy LaFave's street-smart looks. While he may appear to be a rough-and-tumble biker, the original songs that come from the depth of his being are undiluted love-song lullabies. Maybe Jimmy acquired that hard-edged look from the type of work he did before finding music—managing bars, driving truck, and working on a pipeline. Perhaps the lyrics he is famous for are influenced by a loving mother who paid for his first guitar with Green Stamps. His most recent CD, *Buffalo Return to the Plains*, was recorded at Cedar Creek studios in South Austin, and has won critical acclaim. Life in Austin, says Jimmy, is not bad. He's got a horse, a woman friend, a Chevy van, and a dog that likes to snooze at his feet.

Lake Austin Spa Resort

Sweet Potato Crab Cakes and Rémoulade

Located 20 miles from downtown Austin, the Lake Austin Spa Resort takes full advantage of its serene and lovely setting on the banks of the Colorado River. Guests can row or paddle on the river, hike, mountain bike, meditate in the garden by the water, or nap in the hammocks hung from the old oak trees that spread across the grounds. Chef Terry Conlan, author of *Lone Star Cuisine*, prepares meals that are bright, fresh, healthy and lowfat. Much of the produce served is grown at the spa's organic gardens.

Crab cakes:
- 2 cups Dungeness or Alaskan crabmeat, cleaned and broken into small pieces
- ½ large sweet potato
- ½ large white potato
- 1 large egg, beaten
- 2 egg whites, beaten
- 1 teaspoon orange juice concentrate
- 2 teaspoons brown sugar
- ½ teaspoon grated lime zest
- 1 tablespoon lime juice
- 4 tablespoons minced green onion
- 1 garlic clove, minced
- 2 tablespoons minced parsley
- 2 tablespoons finely minced celery
- 1 teaspoon grated orange zest
- ½ teaspoon salt

Rémoulade:
- 1 tablespoon finely minced red bell pepper
- 1 tablespoon finely minced parsley
- 1 cup nonfat sour cream
- ½ cup nonfat mayonnaise
- 2 tablespoons Dijon or Creole mustard
- 1 garlic clove, minced
- 1 tablespoon horseradish
- 1 teaspoon fresh dill weed
- juice of one lime

To prepare the crab cakes: Rinse and drain crab, if necessary. Peel and shred potatoes and blanch in boiling water for one minute. Drain and remove excess water from shredded potatoes by pressing between towels.

In a large mixing bowl, combine all ingredients for crab cakes. Chill for 1–2 hours.

Meanwhile, to prepare rémoulade: Combine all ingredients and chill thoroughly.

Remove crabmeat mixture from refrigerator and shape into patties. Coat a nonstick skillet with vegetable spray or use a small amount of clarified butter. Sauté over medium heat until lightly browned, about 3 minutes per side.

Serve crab cakes with rémoulade sauce on the side. Serves 6

Lake Travis Bed and Breakfast

Sail Away Breakfast Soufflé

A cross between a soufflé and a blintz, this breakfast is a great way to start any adventurous day. It is made the night before, so you can greet the winds early.

8	ounces cream cheese, softened
1	cup cottage cheese
2	egg yolks
1	tablespoon granulated sugar
1	teaspoon vanilla extract
6	eggs
1½	cups sour cream
½	cup orange juice
⅓	cup granulated sugar
1	cup butter or margarine, melted
2	teaspoons baking powder
1	cup flour
	blueberry sauce or fresh blueberries, as a topping

In a mixing bowl, beat together the cream cheese, cottage cheese, egg yolks, sugar, and vanilla. Set aside.

In a blender, purée the eggs, sour cream, orange juice, sugar, butter or margarine, and baking powder, until smooth. Slowly add the flour to the blender, and continue to purée until the batter is smooth.

Butter 8 individual ramekins. Pour half of the batter into the ramekins. Drop the cream cheese mixture by spoonfuls into each of the ramekins. Top each ramekin with the remaining batter. Refrigerate 8 hours or overnight.

Preheat oven to 350°.

Remove ramekins from refrigerator and bake for 45 minutes. Top each blintz or soufflé with blueberry sauce or fresh blueberries. The very creative can also top each soufflé with a sailboat carved from cantaloupe. Serves 8

Lake Travis was created when six dams were built on the Colorado River between the late 1930s and the early 1950s. The lake offers Austinites great possibilities for frolicking in the water. Whether swimming at Hippie Hollow, holding a pole over the cool water in hopes of catching bass or sailing across the bay, Lake Travis is the definition of Texas relaxation. The Lake Travis Bed and Breakfast, a waterfront retreat located just 20 minutes from downtown Austin, looks out at the crystal-clear water from the edge of a cliff. Its guest suites reflect the natural beauty of the surrounding country, and guests soon come to treasure Lake Travis' special brand of relaxation.

Dana Lewis

Pattypan Squash with a Twist

Pattypan, a summer squash, is also known as scalloped squash. Look for this tender squash at the market in late spring. Most are small, just 2 inches across, so adjust the quantity here accordingly, if you can't find larger ones.

4	bacon strips, cut into 1-inch pieces
2	tablespoons olive oil
2	garlic cloves, minced
2	medium or 4 small pattypan squash, diced
2	tablespoons fresh dill
½	bunch broccoli, stemmed and chopped
1	lemon or lime
	salt and pepper to taste
1	tablespoon butter, optional

Hailed by critics for her uncommon speed, soaring jétes, and her crisp lyrical dancing, Dana Lewis has been a principal with Ballet Austin, under the direction of Lambros Lambrou, since 1991. The *Pittsburgh Post-Gazette* described her as a "dangerous dancer—plunging, darting, dazzling at every turn...Lewis feels the freedom to dance on the edge." Dana began her studies in Houston. Upon graduation from the School of American Ballet in New York, she was invited by George Balanchine to join the prestigious New York City Ballet, where she danced for five years. Before joining Ballet Austin, Dana danced with the New World Ballet of Caracas and the distinguished Pittsburgh Ballet Theatre. She has also performed as a guest artist with the Berlin Opera, the Miami Conservatory Ballet, and the Riverside Festival in New York.

In a skillet, cook the bacon over low heat until just cooked though, about 5 minutes. Bacon should not be crisp. Drain oil from pan. Add the olive oil to the same skillet, and sauté the garlic and pattypan squash until the squash is bright in color, about 3 minutes. Stir in the dill and broccoli, and sauté until broccoli is tender-crisp, about 5 minutes more. Squeeze the juice from the lemon or lime over the vegetables. Salt and pepper to taste. Toss with the butter, if desired, and serve immediately. Serves 2–4

David L. Lindsey

Lonesome Dove and Wild Rice

The most abundant dove in Texas can be found in the Hill Country. David says this recipe for morning dove has been in his family for years.

24	dove breasts, skinned
	garlic powder to taste
	fresh parsley, stems removed and finely chopped
1	onion, chopped
1	green pepper, chopped
1	cup chopped celery stalks
3	cups wild rice, cooked according to instructions
3	apples, chopped
1	cup raisins
1	cup chopped pecans
8	slices peppered bacon, cut into thirds

Preheat oven to 350°.

Season the dove with the garlic powder and fresh parsley. In a sauté pan, cook the onion, green pepper, and celery until just barely soft. In a large bowl, combine the cooked wild rice, apples, onion, green pepper, celery, raisins, and pecans. Pour the mixture into a 12x18-inch baking pan. Place the dove breasts on top of the rice mixture. Cover each dove breast with a slice of bacon. Cover the entire pan with tin foil. Bake for 20 minutes. Remove foil and bake for an additional 5-10 minutes, or until the juices run clear when a dove breast is pierced with a fork. Serves 8-10

Anthony L. Lindsey

Writing from his Austin library, David L. Lindsey has penned nine suspense novels, many of which have been set in Texas. Labeled the most literary of Texas crime novelists, he has conducted most of the background research for his books by working with detectives in the Houston Police Department's homicide and intelligence divisions. Other ideas, such as narcotics smuggling and international terrorism, are spurred from his research with the FBI. *Mercy*, published in 1990, enjoyed a stint on the *New York Times'* bestseller list. David's latest book, *Requiem for a Glass Heart*, was purchased by Universal Studios for a feature film starring Demi Moore. He is at work on his tenth novel.

Richard Linklater

Epicurean Slacker's Delight

Go to the H.E.B.
Locate soup aisle
Purchase Country Lentil Cup of Soup
Go home
Boil some water
Pour water, mix, cover
Let sit for 10 to 15 minutes, though it says 7 or 8 on the cup
Enjoy

Webster's dictionary defines the word slacker as *n: one who shirks*. While Austin movie director Richard Linklater may have produced an independent movie by that name, he doesn't live up to the definition himself. Since the 1991 release of *Slacker*, a story of nonconformists living in Austin, Richard has not shirked off his responsibilities. *Dazed and Confused*, released a few years later, further ignited Richard's career and introduced leading man Matthew McConaughey to the world. Since then, bigger budgets and the support of his own production office, Detour Filmproductions, located in Austin and underwritten by Castle Rock Entertainment, may have made it easier to produce quality movies like *Before Sunrise* and *The Newton Boys*, but it doesn't mean Richard is goofing off.

Jerry Long

A Roper's Breakfast

This is a versatile breakfast. You can substitute any number of things for the sausage, including bacon, crabmeat, shrimp, chicken, ham, spinach, or broccoli.

1	pound ground sausage
2	onions, chopped
12	slices bread, crusts removed, cut into ½-inch cubes
1	pound Cheddar cheese, grated
8	eggs, beaten
4	cups milk
1½	teaspoons salt
¼	teaspoon freshly ground pepper
½	teaspoon dry mustard
	chopped jalapeños to taste

Grease a 13x9-inch pan.

Brown the sausage in a sauté pan, breaking the meat apart into small chunks. Remove sausage and set aside. Reserve a tablespoon or so of the sausage drippings in the sauté pan. Add the onion and sauté until soft, about 5 minutes. Add the sausage to the onion, and stir together. Place ½ of the bread in the bottom of the pan. Sprinkle ½ of the sausage mixture and ½ of the cheese over the bread. Repeat layer. In a bowl, combine the eggs, milk, salt and pepper, mustard, and optional jalapeños. Pour over the sausage-bread mixture. Cover and refrigerate at least 24 hours.

Remove from refrigerator 1 hour before serving. Preheat oven to 350°. Bake for 45–50 minutes. Serves 10–12

Jan Spencer

Imagine that you have lost your eyesight and you need to do a simple task, like make breakfast in the morning. Pretty tough. Now imagine, you are sitting on top of a galloping horse with thousands of rodeo fans watching your every move. Your task is to rope a scared and agitated steer. Jerry Long *is* blind and he can lasso the horns or heals of a steer better than many sighted cowboys. When Jerry lost his sight, he thought he'd never ride again, but he got back on a horse and roped one of the first steers he swung his lariat toward. Since then, he's won more than his share of trophy belt buckles. Jerry says, "I've had people tell me that I'm an inspiration and all that, but I rope because I love it." When Jerry isn't riding, he teaches at the Texas School for the Blind in Austin.

James Lovell

In the flash of an explosion aboard Apollo 13, James "Jim" Lovell's dreams of walking on the moon were dashed. The entire country stood glued to their television sets as the Apollo crew, led by Jim, steered their crippled spacecraft back to earth, barely escaping death in deep space. After retiring in 1991, Jim and his wife, Marilyn, moved to Austin's Horseshoe Bay, where he decided to write about the dramatic Apollo 13 flight. Based on that story, *Apollo 13* was a box office slammer. Jim has received a kind of nationwide celebrity not shared by other astronauts, even those who walked on the moon.

Out-of-this-World Crab Strata

Prepare this the night before serving. It's a great dish for company, holiday brunches, or for those lazy Sundays when there is time to savor the wonderful flavors of this great soufflé.

1	tablespoon butter
3	tablespoons bread crumbs
½	pound (about 2 cups) mushrooms, sliced
¼	cup chopped green onions
¼	cup Madeira wine
8	ounces crab, fresh or canned, drained and squeezed
8	slices firm white bread (such as sourdough or French), crusts trimmed
2½	cups milk
4	eggs
2	cups Cheddar cheese, grated
½	teaspoon salt
½	teaspoon dry mustard
	ground black pepper to taste

Butter a 2-quart soufflé dish and dust with bread crumbs. Cut bread into cubes and set aside. Meanwhile in a large frying pan, sauté mushrooms and onions in Madeira over medium heat, stirring continuously, until vegetables are limp. Stir in crabmeat and set aside.

In the soufflé dish, alternate layers of bread cubes and crab mixture, ending with bread cubes.

In a food processor or blender, whirl milk, eggs, cheese, and seasonings until blended. Slowly pour egg mixture over layers in soufflé dish. Cover and refrigerate overnight.

Preheat oven to 325°. Bake uncovered 1½ hours or until a knife inserted comes out clean. Serves 4–6

John Mackovic

Mac Attack Pasta

Coach Mackovic suggests adding other ingredients to his pasta, such as chopped artichoke hearts or Kalamata olives for a salty taste.

12	ounces angel hair pasta
⅓	cup olive oil
2–4	garlic cloves, minced
2–3	tablespoons butter or margarine
2–3	tablespoons pesto
2–3	tablespoons Butter Buds™
⅓	cup chopped fresh parsley
1	tablespoon chopped fresh basil leaves
1	tablespoon chopped fresh oregano leaves
	onion salt and pepper to taste
2	cups seeded and chopped Roma tomatoes
½	cup pine nuts, roasted
4–6	ounces feta cheese
	freshly grated Parmesan cheese

Bring a large pot of water to a boil. Add the pasta and cook until al dente, about 2 minutes. Drain. Meanwhile, heat the olive oil in a large skillet. Add the garlic and butter, and sauté quickly over medium heat. Lower heat, and stir in the pesto, Butter Buds, fresh parsley, basil, oregano, and onion salt and pepper, and cook until just heated through. Toss in the tomatoes, and cook until tomatoes become limp. Place the pasta into a large warmed pasta bowl. Pour the tomato mixture over the pasta. Top with the pine nuts and feta cheese. Serve immediately. Pass the freshly grated Parmesan cheese around the table. Serves 2–4

Before University of Texas Coach John Mackovic became a legend in his own right, he had the rare opportunity to work with a few legendary football players. As a quarterback at Wake Forest, he played in a backfield that included his close friend, the late Brian Piccolo. Later, John spent two years in the 1980s as the quarterback coach for the mythical Tom Landry of the Cowboys. Hired as head coach by UT in 1992, John has changed the look of Texas football by blending a wide-open attack with his philosophy as a former NFL head coach (for the Kansas City Chiefs) and his knowledge of the college game. John and his wife are avid benefactors to various charity organizations in Austin, including the Children's Hospital and St. David's Hospital. He is also a spokesman for the Make-A-Wish Foundation.

Iain Matthews

Veronique's Apple Pie

I often make this pie at night and serve it the next morning. The children feel as if they are getting away with something when they eat apple pie for breakfast! — Veronique Matthews

1	lemon
6–9	Golden Delicious apples, left on the counter for a few days to ripen, peeled and cubed
1½–2	tablespoons apple pie spice
1	prepared 8-inch double pie crust

Preheat oven to 350°.

In a large bowl, squeeze the juice from the lemon. Add the apples and apple pie spice, and mix well. Prepare the pie crust according to instructions. Arrange the apple mixture in the pie crust. Apples should round 1–2 inches above the rim. Top the apples with the remaining pie crust. Bake for 40–45 minutes. The crust should just begin to brown and the apples should be bubbling in the crust. Makes 1 pie

His birth certificate may say he's from England, but his music and lyrics are rooted purely in Austin, Texas. After performing and recording in his native land for decades, Iain Matthews is now in the midst of a creative rebirth in his adopted home. Iain's insight into Texas can be found on his latest album, *The Dark Ride*, and in such songs as *The Ballad of Gruene Hall*, about the oldest dance hall in the Lone Star state, and *Rooted to the Spot*, an authentic honky-tonk rocker.

In 1993, the *Austin Chronicle* voted Iain's *Skeleton Keys* one the top five Austin albums of the year. And luckily for his fans, Iain says, "I've always felt the best part of my life is yet to come."

Ed Mayberry

Mayberry Applesauce Cake

Mayberry Applesauce Cake has been passed down through my family from at least as far back as my great-grandmother, who was born in 1884. Some of my best memories are of listening to the older members of my family tell their stories of old-time radio, war, the great depression, and farm-life. —Ed Mayberry

- 2 cups sifted all-purpose flour
- 1 teaspoon baking soda
- ½ teaspoon salt
- 1 teaspoon cinnamon
- ½ teaspoon ground cloves
- 1 cup coarsely chopped pecans
- ½ cup raisins
- ½ cup shortening
- 1 cup sugar
- 2 egg yolks
- 1½ cups unsweetened applesauce

Preheat oven to 350°.

Grease a 9x5x3-inch loaf pan. In a mixing bowl, combine the flour, baking soda, salt, cinnamon, and cloves. Stir in the pecans and raisins. In a large bowl, cream together the shortening and sugar. Add the egg yolks, and beat well. Alternate adding the flour mixture and the applesauce to the creamed sugar mixture. Beat well after each addition. Pour the batter into the prepared loaf pan and bake for 50 minutes. Makes 1 loaf

What do Paul McCartney, Al Gore, Stevie Ray Vaughan, Yoko Ono, and Lady Bird Johnson have in common? Over the years they have all been interviewed by Ed Mayberry. Ed has been broadcasting news, spinning records, and interviewing his heroes since 1971. Also somewhat of a private investigator, Ed tracked down the couple on the cover of the twenty-year-old Woodstock album to find out what had become of their lives. The curious Ed says he would have liked to have interviewed Albert Einstein, Curly from *The Three Stooges*, and his great-grandfather, John Mayberry. Ed was the co-host with Cecilia Nasti on Austin's 107.1 KGSR morning show, airing cutting-edge adult rock.

Delbert McClinton

Sauced on Tequila Shrimp

This shrimp entrée is best served on rice, but can also be served over pasta.

- 1½ pounds large (26 to 30 count) shrimp, peeled and deveined
- ¼ cup fresh lime juice
- ¼ cup tequila
- ¼ cup water
- ¼ cup minced onion
- 1 tablespoon olive oil
- dash of salt
- 1 lime, quartered, for garnish
- fresh cilantro sprigs, for garnish (optional)

Delbert McClinton once said, "When I die, they'll say I was best known for teaching John Lennon to play the harmonica." Not so, any more. Delbert will be remembered for the sultry, vigorous voice that may be difficult to categorize, but has earned him a mantle packed full of awards. He is the recipient of a Grammy award with Bonnie Raitt for Best **Rock** Duet; and Grammy nominations for Best **Country** Vocal recorded with Tanya Tucker, and Best **Blues** Album for his *Live From Austin* release. Although Delbert now lives in Nashville, his unique sound was cultured in his native Texas. Growing up in Lubbuck and Fort Worth, and spending later years in Austin, Delbert says he barely remembers a day when he wasn't singing.

Prepare the coals for grilling. Place the shrimp in a shallow glass dish. In a small bowl, combine the lime juice, tequila, water, minced onion, olive oil, and salt. Pour the marinade over the shrimp, and let sit for at least 10–15 minutes. Stir occasionally. Remove shrimp from marinade, reserving the marinade. Thread the shrimp onto skewers, so the shrimp can lie flat on the grill. Pour the marinade into a saucepan, and bring to a boil. Reduce heat, and simmer for 5 minutes. Set aside.

Adjust the grill to 4–6 inches above the coals. Coat the grill with vegetable cooking spray. Arrange the shrimp skewers on the grill, and cook until shrimp is opaque, about 3 minutes per side.

Remove the shrimp from the skewers, and arrange over the rice or pasta. Pour the sauce over, and garnish with the lime wedges and fresh cilantro sprigs. Serve immediately. Serves 4

Red McCombs

Go to Hell Prime Rib

The name Go To Hell Prime Rib *came from a friend of mine who had his knife ready to cut off his second big rib, when he was admonished by his wife for eating so much red meat. His response was, "Go to hell!" and he continued slicing the rib.*

The size of the prime rib doesn't matter, but I have always enjoyed cooking larger sizes with at least six to eight ribs. I like to put on a little show for my guests by breaking the salt off the prime rib in their presence with a hammer. This always seems to whet their appetites. And the aroma is to die for. —Red McCombs

- 1 prime rib roast
- your favorite red meat seasonings
- 4 tablespoons Worcestershire sauce
- 3 packages rock salt

Preheat oven to 500°.

Season the prime rib to taste, including the Worcestershire sauce. Cover the bottom of a roasting pan with rock salt, and sprinkle with water to dampen. Place the prime rib on the bed of rock salt. Pour a mountain of rock salt, at least 2 packages, over the rib to completely cover the meat. The meat shouldn't touch anything but salt. Sprinkle the rock salt with water just to dampen.

Cook the prime rib for 12 minutes per pound. To serve, break the hardened salt from the meat with a hammer, and discard. Pick off the few remaining salt flakes, and serve. Serve ½ pound of meat per guest.

Red McCombs is on a trajectory headed up, fast, with no end in sight. The Spur, Texas-native began his career in 1950, selling cars in Corpus Christi, after attending Southwestern University and the University of Texas. Within a decade, he owned a dealership, Red McCombs Automotive. Along with the original dealership, Red is also active in the ownership of thirty auto franchises, and he is a partner in ten other dealerships. Red brought the San Antonio Spurs to his hometown in 1972, and owned the team until recently. He and his wife, Charline Hamblin, have three daughters and eight grandchildren. Charline and Red reside in San Antonio, when not attending to their ranch in the Texas Hill Country or their home in Puerta Vallarta.

God created the world, and master storyteller James Michener recreated it in his spellbinding books of faraway lands. A foundling, James was raised in the Bucks County Poorhouse until he was adopted by Quaker parents, Edwin and Mabel Michener. At fifteen, he began writing a sports column for the Doylestown, Pennsylvania, newspaper. During school breaks, James hitchhiked and rode boxcars across the country, visiting forty-five states by the time he was twenty. After graduating from college, James studied in Europe. In 1942, he enlisted in the Navy and traveled extensively in the South Pacific. His first book, *Tales of the South Pacific*, was published when he was forty and won a Pulitzer Prize. Since then, the Austin resident has written books about places and people around the world, including bestsellers such as *Hawaii*, *Poland*, *Centennial*, *Mexico*, *Alaska*, and *Texas*.

James Michener

James Michener's Beef Bourguignon

This classic French dish warms the soul in winter. We suggest cozying up to a fire with a plateful and one of Mr. Michener's novels. And remember, the better the wine, the better the stew.

- 4 slices bacon
- 2 pounds sirloin tip roast, cut into 1-inch cubes
- 12 whole small onions
- 4 beef bouillon cubes
- 4 bay leaves
- ½ teaspoon dried thyme
- salt and pepper to taste
- 1 garlic clove, minced
- 1 bottle Burgundy wine
- ¼ pound fresh mushrooms, sliced
- 2 tablespoons butter
- tapioca or cornstarch

Cook the bacon in a large Dutch oven until crisp. Remove bacon and crumble. Drain the fat from the pot, leaving a tablespoon or so. Add beef and onion to the bacon drippings, and cook until the beef is browned. Dissolve the bouillon cubes in 4 cups hot water. Add the bouillon to the beef mixture. Add 3½ cups wine. Cook on low, stirring occasionally, for 2 hours. Add bay leaves, thyme, salt, pepper, and garlic. Replenish the wine, as needed. Cook on low for 1 more hour.

Meanwhile, sauté the mushrooms in the butter. Add the mushrooms to the meat mixture at the end of the third hour. If necessary, add more wine. Skim off any fat from the surface. Cook for an additional ½ hour. Thicken the sauce with tapioca or cornstarch, if necessary. Add the crumbled bacon, and serve. Serves 4–6

Ed Miller

A Scot's Dutch Witloof by Way of Texas

This dish makes it worth your time to seek out Belgian endive.

2	pounds (6 medium) potatoes, peeled and cut into quarters
1–2	tablespoons butter
¼	cup milk
¼	teaspoon grated nutmeg
	salt and pepper to taste
1	head Belgian endive
10	thin slices cooked ham or turkey
½	pound (about 2 cups) grated Edam cheese
	Parmesan cheese, grated for topping
2	tablespoons butter

Preheat oven to 350°.

Boil potatoes in large saucepan until they are tender, about 20–25 minutes. Drain well, return to the pan, and mash with a masher, fork, or electric mixer. Add butter, milk, nutmeg, and salt and pepper. Mix thoroughly. Set aside.

Meanwhile, steam the endive for a few minutes, drain and separate. Wrap each piece of endive in a slice of ham or turkey, and place them in a buttered casserole. Cover them with grated Edam cheese, then mashed potatoes. Finally, sprinkle the Parmesan cheese on top with some *wee bits* of butter. Bake for 20 minutes, or until the top gets a golden crust... *Enjoy.* Serves 6

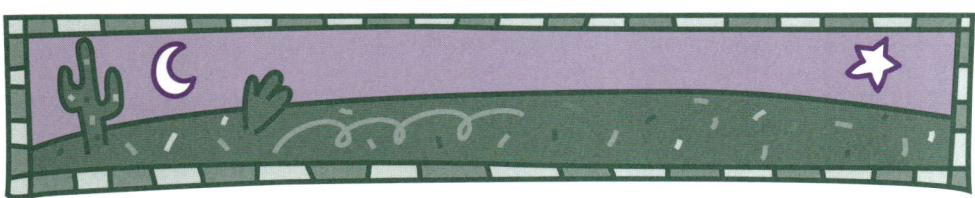

Leaving his home of Edinburgh, Scotland, in 1968—Ed Miller intended to do graduate work in geography for a year or so in the United States. He ended up studying folklore at the University of Texas. In the meantime, Austin has become Ed's home base and Ed has become something of a Scottish ambassador to Texas. His repertoire of Scottish folk revival tunes, including ageless ballads and the songs of Robert Burns, and contemporary folk music give the audience a glimpse of the ebb and flow of Scottish life. Ed performs throughout North America, and hosts a folk music show on National Public Radio that is recorded at Austin's KUT-FM. He has recorded three albums, *Border Background, Home and Away,* and *Scottish Voice.*

Abra Moore

Andrew Long

Abra Moore, a former member of Poi Dog Pondering, has found a home, at last, in Austin. Raised in Hawaii, Abra spent years on the road with her band before taking a sabbatical to travel and soak up the jazz culture of Europe. She then moved to Austin where Jimmy Lafave called her the "most original singer/songwriter in town." His admiration and support led to a record contract with Bohemia Beat and the release of *Sing*, a stunning solo debut. Abra told *Texas Monthly*, "A part of my soul is Hawaiian, but Austin is my home. It still feels quaint and safe. It's easy living, for an artist."

More Mango Pie, Please

I was raised in Hawaii, where mangoes grow like weeds. We spent many weekends gathering them up, peeling and preparing them for pies. —Abra Moore

Pie crust:
- 2 cups all-purpose flour
- 1/3 teaspoon salt
- 1 cup butter, chilled
- 6 tablespoons cold water

Pie filling:
- 5 cups seeded, peeled, and sliced mangoes
- 1/2 cup packed brown sugar or honey
- 1/3 teaspoon salt
- 1 tablespoon cornstarch
- 1/3 teaspoon cinnamon
- juice from 1 lemon
- 1 teaspoon vanilla extract

To prepare the crust: Combine the flour and salt in a mixing bowl. Using a pastry blender or your fingers, cut in the butter until the mixture is crumbly. Add the water, stirring until the mixture holds together. Form the dough into a ball. Roll the pastry out on a flat, floured surface. Cut out 2 crusts from the dough. Line a 9-inch pie plate. Reserve the other pie crust to cover the top.

Preheat oven to 350°.

In a large bowl, combine the mango, brown sugar or honey, salt, cornstarch, cinnamon, fresh-squeezed lemon juice, and vanilla extract. Mix well. Pour the filling into the pie crust. Cover the pie with the second pie crust and flute the edges. Make a few slits in the top of the pie. Bake until the top is golden, about 40–45 minutes. Makes 1 pie

Azie Taylor Morton

A Treasure of a Tamale Pie

1	tablespoon olive oil
1	cup chopped onion
1	cup chopped green bell pepper
¾	pound ground beef
2	8-ounce cans seasoned tomato sauce
1	12-ounce can corn kernels, drained
1	cup chopped ripe olives
1	garlic clove, minced
1	tablespoon granulated sugar, optional
1	teaspoon salt
2–3	teaspoons chili powder
	freshly ground black pepper to taste
1½	cups grated sharp Cheddar cheese

Topping:
¾	cup yellow cornmeal
½	teaspoon salt
2	cups cold water
1	tablespoon butter or margarine

Preheat oven to 375°.

Grease a large casserole. Heat the vegetable oil in a large skillet. Sauté the onion and green bell pepper until the onion is soft, about 5–7 minutes. Add the ground beef, and brown. Add the tomato sauce, corn, olives, garlic, sugar, salt, chili powder, and pepper. Simmer over low heat until thick, about 20–25 minutes. Add the cheese, and stir until cheese is melted. Spoon the meat mixture into the casserole.

To prepare the topping: In a saucepan, stir the cornmeal and salt into the water. Cook over low heat until thick, about 10 minutes. Add the butter and mix well. Spoon the cornmeal topping over the meat mixture in 3 lengthwise strips. Bake for 40 minutes. Serves 6–8

Azie Taylor Morton was born a leader. She began her professional career as a cum laude business education graduate from Austin's Huston-Tillotson College teaching delinquent girls. Her efforts were recognized when she was awarded "Teacher of the Year." Azie then became interested in politics, and she began pouring her considerable energy toward the Democratic Party. She has held many prestigious posts, most notably as the U.S. Treasurer under Jimmy Carter. To this day, Azie is the only African-American to have held that post. Azie now travels from her home in Austin to emerging democracies in Africa and South America to monitor elections for the United Nations. She also brings her organizational and financial expertise to the Austin Parks Foundation as an advisory board member.

Michael Martin Murphey

Michael Martin Murphey's singing career began modestly. At sixteen, he performed as a singing cowboy and wrangler at the Sky Ranch in Lewisville, Texas. His first album, *Geronimo's Cadillac*, recorded while living in Austin, established Michael as a singing cowboy off the ranch. Now, twenty-four albums later, and famous for his tune *Wildfire*, Michael's passion for the cowboy life extends beyond his music. He created the character "Murph" for the *Lonesome Dove* television series. In addition, he wrote the screenplay, coordinated the soundtrack, and starred in the film *Hard Country*. Michael currently lives on a ranch in New Mexico with his horses, wife, and children.

Grandma's Ham Hallelujah

6–8	medium potatoes, peeled and sliced thin
	salt and pepper to taste
¼–½	cup flour
4	tablespoons butter, cut into slivers
½	pound Canadian bacon or ham, sliced thin
¼	cup grated cheese (Cheddar, Gruyère, or Fontina are good choices)
2	cups 2% or nonfat milk

Preheat oven to 350°. Spray a 2-quart casserole with vegetable cooking spray.

Place a thin layer of potatoes on the bottom of the casserole. Sprinkle with salt and pepper, flour, and butter slivers. Follow with a thin layer of Canadian bacon or ham. Continue with several layers, ending with Canadian bacon. Sprinkle the grated cheese over the top. Pour the milk over the cheese. Bake until the cheese is crispy, about 1 hour. Remove from oven and let sit for 10 minutes before serving. Serves 6–8

Cecilia Nasti

A Woman on the Verge of Herbed Orzo

For a Texas flair, add a large jalapeño pepper (seeded and sliced) to the garlic and ginger. You can also substitute fresh cilantro for the basil, and toasted pecans for the pine nuts. —Cecilia Nasti

1	16-ounce package orzo
¼	cup extra-virgin olive oil
4	large garlic cloves, minced
1½	inches fresh ginger root, peeled and minced
½	cup fresh sweet basil leaves, finely chopped
⅓	cup pine nuts, lightly toasted in a dry pan over high heat
½	cup fresh Italian parsley leaves, finely chopped
	salt and pepper to taste
	fresh basil leaves for garnish

Prepare the orzo according to the instructions. Drain, and transfer to a serving dish. Keep warm.

Meanwhile, in a small skillet, heat the olive oil. Sauté the garlic and ginger until the garlic browns slightly. Remove from heat and let cool. Drain the oil from the garlic and ginger. Add the basil, pine nuts, and parsley. Spoon the basil-pine nut mixture into the orzo. Toss gently. Season with salt and pepper. Garnish with basil leaves. Serves 6

Cecilia Nasti says she was meant to be a Texan, but she was born by some cruel act of irony in the Midwest. Even as a little girl growing up outside of Chicago, she soaked up any book, movie, or bit of news that came from the Lone Star state. So after graduating from college, Cecilia jumped at the chance to move to Lockhart, Texas, to work as a VISTA volunteer. In Lockhart she began her career in radio, working as a volunteer news anchor. A few years and a few jobs later, Cecilia achieved her goal—a radio position in Austin. While at Austin's public radio station, KUT-FM, Cecilia produced two nationally syndicated programs. Today she has evolved from a full-time news director into the brave and witty co-host of *KGSR in the Morning*. She lives outside Austin in an old house on two acres with her Sweet Baboo, two cats, and a dog.

Gary P. Nunn

Gary P. Nunn captured that down mood that only Austin can cure when he penned the classic *London Homesick Blues*, which first appeared on *Viva Terlingua*, Jerry Jeff Walker's million-selling album, and was adopted as the theme song for *Austin City Limits*. Gary has shown a certain gift from the beginning of his music career. He led the Lost Gonzo Band, backing up Michael Martin Murphey and Jerry Jeff Walker. He has composed tunes recorded by Willie Nelson, Rosanne Cash, and many others. Since being on his own, Gary has released two CDs, *Totally Guacamole* and *Roadtrip*. He performs with his band, The Sons of the Bunkhouse, forty-eight weekends a year throughout Texas and the Southwest. He has resisted offers to relocate to Nashville, preferring to promote the growing music industry in Texas, where he enjoys a near folk hero status.

Züricher Geschnitzeltes

You may add your favorite spices to the meat sauce. It serves well with noodles, mashed potatoes, or rice. Bon Appétit, Ya'll. —*Gary P. Nunn*

2	pounds veal, cut into 1-inch cubes
1	teaspoon each salt and pepper
¼	cup flour
6	tablespoons butter or margarine
1	onion, chopped
1	garlic clove, minced, or more to taste
3½	cups (10 ounces) fresh mushrooms, sliced
1¼	cups (10 ounces) white wine
1	beef bouillon cube
	salt and pepper to taste
½	cup heavy cream

Place veal, salt and pepper, and flour in paper bag, and shake to lightly coat. Melt butter over medium-high heat in large, heavy skillet. Add veal, stirring constantly so that it does not burn, and cook. Remove when meat is cooked through. Keep warm.

In the same skillet sauté onion, garlic, and mushrooms, lowering heat slightly. Add white wine, crumbled bouillon cube, salt and pepper and simmer on low heat for about 5 minutes. Add cream, stir very well, and simmer for about 1 minute. Add reserved meat and simmer for about 5 minutes, stirring frequently.

Serve immediately over potatoes, pasta, or rice. Serves 6

Joe Nick Patoski

My Ladies' Greek Chicken

From a son's perspective, there is usually no way to beat Mom's home-cooking, especially when your Mom is Greek. But in my case, my Nebraska-bred wife, Kris, has accomplished the trick by learning from the master herself, then adding a few variations, specifically the garlic. —Joe Nick Patoski

- ¼ cup olive oil
- 3 garlic cloves, minced
- 1 medium onion, finely chopped
- 1 3-pound chicken, cut into serving pieces, rinsed and patted dry
- 1½ pounds fresh tomatoes, peeled and chopped
- 1 teaspoon salt
- ½ teaspoon freshly ground pepper
- 3 cinnamon sticks
- 4½ cups boiling water, divided
- 2 cups white rice, rinsed

Heat the olive oil in a large skillet, and sauté the garlic and onion for a few minutes. Add the chicken pieces and cook over medium heat, turning once, until skin is browned. Add the tomatoes, salt and pepper, cinnamon sticks and ½ cup boiling water. Cover and simmer for 45 minutes. Stir in the rice and remaining 4 cups boiling water. Cover and simmer for 20 more minutes, or until the rice is soft. Serves 4–6

He's a half-breed Greek boy, who may know as much about the Austin and Texas music scene as anyone. Joe Nick Patoski is a senior editor at *Texas Monthly* magazine, co-author of *Stevie Ray Vaughan: Caught in the Crossfire*, and *Selena: Coma la Flor*, both published by Little, Brown. Joe Nick has contributed articles to *Rolling Stone*, the *Village Voice*, and *Creem*, among other music publications. He is a former music columnist for the *Austin American-Statesman*. As long as he is able to crawl, he will be an avid Barton Springs swimmer.

Tom Penders

When Tom Penders took charge of the University of Texas' basketball team in 1998, he put his stamp on the Longhorns by calling them the "Runnin' Horns." In the years preceding Tom's arrival, UT fans—the few that remained—were used to seeing the Longhorns plod up and down the floor and a mediocre record. But all that changed with the fast-paced game that Tom inspired. The team started winning games and conferences, and attendance more than doubled. Under the Stratford, Connecticut-native's direction, the "Runnin' Horns" have made six NCAA tournament appearances, the best in school history. In Austin, the Connecticut Yankee is a popular figure. Tom assists with several basketball camps for children, and volunteers for just about everything, including judging a cow chip throwing contest, *if* it's for a good cause.

Coach Penders' Breakfast Tacos

Coach Penders' Breakfast Tacos are a fast, healthy, and low-fat way to start the day.

½	tablespoon canola oil
½	cup chopped onion
½	cup chopped red bell pepper
2	cartons Eggbeaters or another egg substitute
6	flour tortillas
	hot sauce to taste

In a skillet over medium-low heat, heat the canola oil. Add the onion and bell pepper, and sauté until limp, about 5–7 minutes. Add the Eggbeaters, and cook, stirring frequently, until eggs are firm. Top the eggs with hot sauce. Microwave the flour tortillas for 30 seconds. Wrap the eggs in tortillas, and rush out the door to basketball practice. Serves 2–4

Jo Carol Pierce

Twice-Naked Pesto

I call this pesto Texican Pesto Verde, but my husband, Juke, calls it Twice-Naked Pesto for reasons he cannot or will not explain. Another thing, Juke likes to add Parmesan cheese, but I don't. Serve the pesto hot or cold on pasta, garnished with whole roasted pumpkin seeds. You can also serve it on tortilla rounds. Or use it as a dip. —Jo Carol Pierce

- 1–4 garlic cloves, chopped
- 2 cups chopped fresh cilantro
- ¼ cup roasted pumpkin seeds
- ¼ cup sesame oil or olive oil
- 2 tablespoons lime juice
- 1–2 roasted, seeded, skinned, and chopped Anaheim peppers
- Parmesan cheese to taste, optional
- salt and pepper to taste

Place all of the ingredients in a blender, and blend until smooth. Will keep in a sealed jar in the refrigerator for 1 week. Makes 2 cups

Jo Carol Pierce says she spent her early life as a "'lonesome polecat in Prairie Dog Town," also known as Lubbuck, Texas. Several years ago she won Best Songwriter and Best CD at the Austin Music Awards, became a grandmother, and caught the eye of artist musician and big old rough boy, Guy Juke, whom she'd had a crush on for about twenty years. She's proud of appearing on stage at the Lincoln Center in *Chippy*, riding freight trains with Jesse Taylor, her CD *Bad Girls Upset by the Truth*, her daughter, Elyse Gilmore Yates, her husband, and her three darling ex-husbands.

Toni Price

Stevie Jo Lake Photography

Toni Price is a small woman with a big, power-house of a voice. The music that climbs out of her soul resonates like a stand-up bass. At the 1995–1996 Austin Music Awards, Toni's name appeared at the top of the list in nearly every category that applied. She was named best female vocalist and best blues musician. She garnered top awards for her album *Hey*, and her songs *Tumbleweed*, *Hey*, and *Too Much Coffee* placed first, second and fifth, respectively. Toni, who has lived in Austin since 1989, has spent many Tuesday afternoons as the lead musician at the Continental Club's happy hour. Toni humbly calls herself a "singer of songs and a mother of two." Amber and Della call her Mom.

Barn Dance Potluck Potato Salad

Toni says, "I love to cook, but I ain't crazy about cleaning up…"

6	medium (2 pounds) whole potatoes
1	cup chopped celery
½	cup chopped onion
⅓	cup relish or chopped pickles
1¼	cups mayonnaise
2	teaspoons sugar
2	teaspoons celery seed
2	teaspoons vinegar
2	teaspoons Dijon mustard
1½	teaspoons salt
2	eggs, hard-boiled, peeled and chopped

Boil the whole potatoes in a large pot of water until tender, about 30 minutes. Drain and cool. Peel the potatoes and cut into 1-inch cubes. Put the potatoes in a large bowl. Add the celery, onion, and relish or chopped pickle, and mix well. In a small bowl, combine the mayonnaise, sugar, celery seed, vinegar, Dijon mustard, and salt. Whisk until blended. Add the mayonnaise mixture to the potatoes, and toss lightly to coat potatoes. Add the hard-boiled eggs, and mix gently. Cover and chill. Serves 8

Jenna Beth Radtke

New Mexico Corn Bake

1½	cups corn kernels, cooked
1	15-ounce can cream-style corn
2	eggs, beaten
½	cup vegetable oil
¾	cup yellow cornmeal
¼	teaspoon garlic powder
½	teaspoon baking powder
½	cup chopped green chiles
¼	cup chopped pimientos
2	cups grated sharp Cheddar cheese

Preheat oven to 350°.

Grease a 13x9-inch pan. In a mixing bowl, combine the corn kernels, cream-style corn, eggs, and vegetable oil. In a separate smaller bowl, combine the cornmeal, garlic powder, and baking powder. Gradually add the dry ingredients to the corn mixture, and mix until just blended. Fold in the green chiles, pimientos, and grated cheese. Pour the mixture into the prepared pan. Bake for 45 minutes. Serves 6–8

Jenna Beth Radtke, owner of Lucy in Disguise with Diamonds and Electric Ladyland in South Austin, is known for her collections of almost anything outrageous or kitsch. Her homes are actually more like "theme museums" with their absolute color coordination and retro decor, and her stores have been featured in newspapers, magazines, television shows, and photo and video shoots. She and her stores have won awards for best wardrobe and costume store. Most Austinites agree that at any given time, at any given event, Jenna Beth is always the best dressed person in the room—or at least the most noticeable.

Brenda Ladd

In the exploding jazz culture of Texas, Tomás Ramirez is one of its most respected musicians. He has recorded with a variety of groups, including Dan del Santo and Beto y los Fairlanes. He has even crossed the borders of jazz to record with Christopher Cross and Carole King. Tomás arrived in Austin in 1970 with his saxophone in hand, and was soon a member of Jerry Jeff Walker's Lost Gonzo Band. In another six years he started his first jazz band, the Jazzmanian Devils, creators of the album *Thanks for the Good-byes*. The South Texas native has been strongly influenced by the *conjunto* traditions and that sound is reflected on his independent album *Tejazz*.

Tomás Ramirez

Migas al Chino

- 2 eggs, beaten into submission
- 1 tablespoon tamari or soy sauce
- 2 tablespoons vegetable oil (or olive, peanut, or sesame oil)
- 1 corn tortilla, cut into 8 equal pieces (Make sure all pieces are *exactly* equal, or you will die.)
- 3 garlic cloves, minced
- 1 tablespoon grated fresh ginger root
- ½ tablespoon whole comino (cumin)
- ¼ cup bok choy, diced on the diagonal
- ¼ cup chopped onion
- ¼ cup chopped tomatoes
- 6 snow peas, diced on the diagonal
- 6 bamboo shoots, diced
- 1 fresh jalapeño, diced
- 2 tablespoons finely chopped green bell pepper
- salt and pepper to taste

In a small bowl, combine the eggs and tamari. Beat until frothy. Set aside. Pour the oil into a wok or deep frying pan heated over medium heat—the deeper the pan, the better. Add tortilla pieces and fry until crisp. Remove, and set aside. Add the garlic, ginger, and comino, and sauté for about 15 seconds. Add the eggs, coating the bottom of the pan and the tortilla pieces. Add the bok choy, onion, tomatoes, snow peas, bamboo shoots, jalapeño, and green pepper. Cook, stirring often, until eggs are firm. Salt and pepper to taste. Serves 1

John Randall

The Most Famous Hot Sauce In Texas

The reason John wins hot sauce competitions year after year: "I grow the tomatoes myself. Another important consideration is a sharp knife and uniform cutting of the veggies so that each piece stands on its own identity. Many people end up mashing ingredients with dull knives instead of cutting them." —John Randall

- 6 fresh tomatoes
- ¼ yellow onion, finely diced
- ¼ red onion, finely diced
- ¼ white onion, finely diced
- 2 green onions, finely diced
- ½ bunch cilantro, coarsely chopped
- 4 pickled jalapeños, finely chopped
- 4 fresh jalapeños, finely chopped
- 8 serrano peppers, finely chopped
- 1 tablespoon salt
- 1 teaspoon cayenne pepper
- 1 teaspoon fresh garlic purée

Prick tomatoes with a fork and blanch in boiling water for a few seconds. Peel. To seed tomatoes, slice in half around the middle section. Gently squeeze tomatoes over sink, extracting the seeds. Chop tomatoes coarsely in food processor and place in medium bowl. Add the remaining ingredients, mix thoroughly, and refrigerate for 4 hours. Place a fire extinguisher within reach. Makes 3 cups

John Randall may not fit the description of a celebrity, but he's cooked for plenty of them. He was Lady Bird Johnson's personal chef; Ann Richards is a devotee of his hot sauce; and, in his two decades of cooking around Austin, he's fed just about every big wig in town. He is currently the chef de cuisine at Austin's Green Pastures Restaurant, listed as one of James Beard's "100 Greatest Restaurants in the World." John consistently places among the top three in the annual Travis County Farmers' Market Hot Sauce Festival, the largest event of its kind with more than 400 entries.

Dan Rather

On November 22, 1963, in Dallas, Dan Rather broke the news of the death of President John F. Kennedy to the nation. Since that time, he has been in the thick of headline news—covering such stories for CBS as the revolt in Tiananmen Square, the Persian Gulf War, the fall of the Berlin Wall, and the front lines of the siege of Sarajevo. The well-traveled Huntsville native says he would like to live "anywhere the stars at night are big and bright, where the skies by day are blue and sunny, amid green forests and clean water—namely, in Texas." When the Emmy award-winner isn't chasing the news around the globe, he can be found at his place in the Hill Country.

My Mom's Vinegar Pie

Vinegar pie is a Texas dessert and was immensely popular during the Depression. Spices may be added to the hot vinegar syrup—cinnamon, nutmeg, mace, or allspice—singly or in combination. —Dan Rather

1	9-inch pie crust (with lattice top, optional)
1	cup cider vinegar
1¾	cups water
½–2	cups brown sugar or granulated sugar, amount depending upon the times
2	tablespoons butter
¾	cup all-purpose flour, or more

Preheat oven to 450°.

Line a 9-inch pie plate with the pastry dough. Chill. In a saucepan, combine the vinegar, water, and sugar. Bring to a boil, and boil for 3 minutes, stirring. Lower heat, add butter, and stir until butter is melted. Mix the flour with just enough cold water to make a smooth paste. Slowly add the flour to the hot syrup, stirring as the flour is added. Cook, stirring constantly, until the syrup is thickened and smooth. Pour the syrup into the pie shell. Lay on lattice strips, if desired. Press ends of strips securely to edge of crust. Crimp edges of crust. Bake for 10 minutes. Lower heat to 350°, and bake 25 more minutes. Serve hot or cold. Serves 6–8

Jan Reid

Rosemary Garlic Roasted Potatoes

Rosemary grows wild in the south of France, and the hardy and fragrant shrub thrives in strikingly similar climate and soil—the Texas Hill Country. In fact, about the only perennial that seems better suited to Austin's patchy shade, erratic weather, and limestone-bedded soil is the sorry juniper. Every yard and nearby kitchen deserves a rosemary plant. It's even ornamental.

Potatoes rate almost equal billing to tomatoes in the spring vegetable garden. The vining plants are easy to grow, handsome in a row, and produce in large quantity. Freshly dug potatoes, when compared to even the best available in supermarket bins, offer a stunning surprise of taste and texture.

These two star ingredients invite a more-is-good variation on a theme by noted Austin chef, author, and teacher Ann Clark. Add heat, fresh garlic, and olive oil, and you have the perfect complement to grilled beef, lamb, or fish. —Jan Reid

new red, small white, or blue potatoes
abundant fresh rosemary
cloves of fresh garlic
virgin olive oil
freshly ground black pepper
salt, preferably sea or coarse kosher

Preheat oven to 400°. Cut the unpeeled potatoes in half, and thinly slice into crescents. Break off a couple of branches from your rosemary bush, strip the leaves, and chop leaves coarsely. Peel and chop the garlic, not too finely—the roasted garlic nuggets add pops of pleasure to the mix of flavors. In a large mixing bowl, pour enough olive oil to cover the rosemary and garlic, with salt and copious black pepper.

Add the potatoes, and stir until the slices are well coated. Spread potatoes out on a roasting pan. Bake for 15 to 20 minutes, turning potatoes with a spatula two or three times to prevent sticking. You may judge when they are done by the crispness and color—golden, but not brown.

Don't underestimate how much will be consumed, and with dinner guests, expect some crowding in the kitchen. Aroma serves the first course.

As irony would have it, it wasn't a musician who helped forever change the course of the Austin music scene, but a writer. In 1974, Jan Reid wrote *The Improbable Rise of Redneck Rock*, detailing the merging of country and rock music styles. The book was the inspiration for *Austin City Limits*, the longest-running show on PBS. The show and the growing number of musicians based in Austin helped give the city its moniker, "the third coast of music." Jan, a founding contributor of *Texas Monthly*, has gone on to publish wide-ranging essays and articles with *Esquire, Men's Journal*, and other national publications. The Austin writer, a recipient of grants from the National Endowment for the Arts and the Texas Commission on the Arts, has since published other books, including *Vain Glory* and *Deerinwater*.

George Reiff is involved in two of Austinites' favorite pastimes—music and food. Some days he earns a living as a bass player and songwriter. Other days he is a pastry chef. Once in awhile, George says he gets confused and, "Sometimes I show up for work dressed improperly!" Luckily, George works at tony Jeffrey's restaurant, where the clientele wear anything from T-shirts to tuxedos, so George can create his delicacies, whatever his attire. He also keeps busy playing with other Austin musicians and friends, among them Michael Fracasso, Charlie Sexton, Cotton Mather, and Johnny Reno.

George Reiff

Lyle Loved It Tart

Once upon a time, Lyle Lovett happened upon a cafe where I was employed as a pastry chef. I had just come up with this particular dessert which acquired the very unspectacular name of Pistachio and Blood Orange Tart. Lyle had a slice and thus the tart's eternal moniker was born on the spot. —George Reiff

Crust:
- 1½ cups all-purpose flour
- ½ cup pistachios
- ¼ cup granulated sugar
- ¾ cup chilled butter, cut into small cubes
- 1 egg
- 1 egg yolk
- pinch salt

Filling:
- 4 blood oranges
- 4 eggs, beaten
- ½ cup sour cream
- ¼ cup granulated sugar
- blood oranges, peeled, and cut into rounds for garnish
- ½ cup chopped, lightly toasted pistachios for garnish

To prepare the crust: Preheat oven to 375°. Add the flour, pistachios, and sugar to a food processor. Pulse to mix and to coarsely chop the nuts. Add the butter, and pulse until mixture resembles coarse crumbs. Add the egg, egg yolk, and salt, and continue to pulse until the dough just holds together. Do not over process. The dough should be sort of "shaggy." Chill until firm. Roll out the dough. Fit dough into a tart pan, trim, and crimp the edges. Bake crust until golden-brown, about 30–40 minutes.

Meanwhile, to prepare the filling: Grate the zest from 2 oranges, and chop the zest until it is very fine. Transfer the zest to a mixing bowl. Juice all 4 oranges, and add the juice to the zest. Mix well. Whisk the eggs into the juice mixture. In a separate bowl, beat the sour cream and sugar together until well blended. Add the sour cream mixture to the juice mixture. Pour into a saucepan. Cook over low heat, stirring constantly, until the mixture thickens. Do not boil. Chill.

Pour the orange filling into the crust. Lower heat to 300°. Bake for 20 minutes. Cool. Arrange the orange rounds over the tart, overlapping, in circles. Sprinkle the tart with chopped pistachios. Take one long, last look at your beautiful creation, and serve... Makes 1 tart

Mary Lou Retton

Paella to Flip Over

6	skinless chicken thighs
½	teaspoon salt
½	cayenne pepper, divided
2	tablespoons olive oil
1	large onion, chopped
3	garlic cloves, minced
2	cups long-grain white rice
2	15-ounce cans chicken broth
½	cup dry white wine, or dry vermouth
½	teaspoon saffron threads, crumbled
1	14½-ounce can diced tomatoes, drained
1	7-ounce jar marinated artichoke hearts, drained, and coarsely chopped
1	cup sweet peas
¾	pound large shrimp, peeled and deveined
12	large mussels, well scrubbed
	fresh parsley leaves for garnish

Preheat oven to 375°.

Rinse the chicken, and pat dry. Sprinkle with salt and ¼ teaspoon cayenne pepper. Heat the olive oil over medium heat in a large Dutch oven. Cook the chicken until browned, about 6–8 minutes per side. Remove the chicken, and set aside. Sauté the onion and garlic in the remaining oil until the onion is limp, about 5 minutes. Add the rice, and mix well. Stir in the chicken broth, wine, saffron, and the remaining ¼ teaspoon cayenne pepper. Bring to a boil. Reduce heat, and simmer for 10 minutes. Stir in the tomatoes, artichoke hearts, peas, shrimp, mussels, and chicken pieces. Mix well. Cover Dutch oven, and bake paella until the liquid is absorbed, about 35–40 minutes. Let sit 10 minutes before serving. Garnish with fresh parsley leaves. Serves 6

Mary Lou Retton is a national hero, especially to the throngs of little girls who watched the tiny but tough 16-year-old become the first American woman ever to win an Olympic gold medal in gymnastics. But her impact has been felt by more than just those inspired to vault and flip. Mary Lou has influenced many others with her motivational speeches and her example of a normal, happy celebrity home life. Mary Lou is married to financial analyst Shannon Kelley, a former University of Texas quarterback, whom she met while both were students in Austin. Their daughter, Shayla Rae, was born in 1995. Mary Lou stays busy as a commentator for NBC, and she writes a column for *USA Today*.

Ann Richards

Born in Lakeview, Texas, Ann Richards says she learned a silent lesson from her parents that would shape her life: "My parents never wanted me to have to work as hard as they did. But that was all I ever saw them do, and the message I got was that the only things of any real value in life were family and hard work." A perfectionist with a strong Methodist social conscience, Ann has worked hard—as a school teacher, mother of four, Travis County commissioner, state treasurer, and finally as Texas governor—to ensure that Texas is a better place for her six grandchildren and for every Texan. Now, Ann says she truly enjoys a new life away from public office. Currently, she is a senior advisor to the law firm Verner, Liipfert, Bernhard, McPherson & Hand, and lives in Austin.

Firecracker Cornbread

Two of the liveliest things about Texas are its jalapeños and Ann Richards. Here we get the best of both. You can add even more pizzazz to Ann's recipe by including bacon bits, chopped pimiento, or chopped garlic. You decide what and how much.

- ¾ cup milk
- 1 egg, beaten
- 2 tablespoons vegetable oil
- 1½ cups cornbread mix
- 1 tablespoon sugar
- ½ green onion, chopped
- ½ cup creamed corn
- ¼ cup chopped jalapeño peppers
- ¾ cup grated Monterey Jack cheese, or Cheddar cheese, or a combination
- Optional: bacon bits, chopped pimiento, chopped garlic, to taste

Preheat oven to 425°.

Grease an 8-inch square pan. In a mixing bowl, combine the milk, egg, and vegetable oil. Gradually stir in the cornbread mix and sugar until smooth. Add the green onion, creamed corn, and jalapeños. Fold in the grated cheese, and optional ingredients. Pour batter into prepared pan, and bake until golden, about 20–25 minutes. Cool for a few minutes before serving. Serves 8

Charlie Robison

Honey Butter and Jalapeño Dove

If you can get your hands on some of these birds, cooking them à la Robison is well worth your time. This recipe generates grilled fare that's superb.

- 10 cleaned dove
- 10 large fresh jalapeños
- 10 strips bacon
- ½ cup butter, melted
- ¼ cup honey

Stuff each dove with whole jalapeño and wrap with bacon. Fasten bacon with toothpick.

Mix butter and honey together over low heat in a small saucepan. Set aside.

Place doves on covered barbecue grill (should be 6 inches from heat) and cook, turning and basting with honey butter about every 10 minutes, until the birds are nicely browned and cooked through, and when pierced the juices run clear, approximately 25–35 minutes. Serves 6–8

Charlie Robison is currently Bandera's third most famous citizen—and that really ticks him off. Singer-songwriter Robert Earl Keen ranks first. Second is a local policeman convicted of a bank robbery. Not that Charlie has stood still in third place. He turned the cop drama into a song. Such true-life experiences add an honest and unforgettable appeal to Charlie's music, and he is only beginning to hit his stride. In 1995, Charlie released his independent debut album *Bandera*. The suits at Warners Brothers/Reprise Records in Nashville heard a few cuts, and signed him immediately. Watch your back, Robert Earl.

Johnny Rodriguez

In 1968, when Johnny Rodriguez was spending time in jail for goat rustling, his singing caught the ear of a Texas Ranger. The Ranger told Happy Shahan about the young goat rustler and before long, Johnny was singing at Shahan's Alamo Village near Brackettville. There he was discovered by Tom T. Hall, and the rest is country music history. Since then, Johnny has had songs on the country charts consistently for nearly ten years—hits like *Pass Me By*, *Love Put a Song in My Heart*, *North of the Border*, and *Ridin' My Thumb to Mexico*. The second youngest of ten children, Johnny spends his time at home in Austin fishing, playing golf and tennis, horseback riding, and cooking.

Fresh Rodriguez Pico de Gallo

2	fresh, plump tomatoes, cut into quarters
1	white onion, cut into quarters
1	garlic clove
½	cup cilantro leaves
1	poblano pepper, seeded and cut into quarters
½	jalapeño pepper, seeded and cut into quarters
	juice of a lime or lemon
¼	teaspoon salt
¼	teaspoon pepper

Place tomatoes, onions, and cilantro in a food processor and chop vegetables briefly. They should be coarsely chopped and not mushy. Pour into glass bowl.

Chop peppers and garlic in processor until are they finely chopped. Mix with tomato mixture. Stir in citrus juice and salt and pepper. Refrigerate for one hour and serve with chips or with any Mexican-style entrée.

Makes 2 cups

Robert Rodriguez

Desperate for Pecan Pie

For Texans, it is not "mom and apple pie." Pecan pie rules supreme. Robert has shared his own version of this Lone Star manna and it is—almost—worth going to war over.

- 6 tablespoons butter, melted
- 1 cup granulated sugar
- ¾ cup corn syrup
- 3 eggs, beaten
- 1 teaspoon vanilla
- 10 ounces (about 2½ cups) pecans, chopped
- 9-inch pie shell

Preheat oven to 400°.

In a large mixing bowl, blend melted butter and sugar with a wooden spoon. Stir in corn syrup and mix well. Add eggs, stirring until smooth. Stir in vanilla and pecans.

Pour into the pie shell and bake for 45–60 minutes. Makes 1 pie

He is not just the independent director whose film *El Mariachi* catapulted him from Austin into the hearts of Hollywood's rich and powerful. Or *just* the genius behind *Desperado* and *From Dusk Till Dawn*. Robert Rodriguez is a cartoonist, whose strip *Los Hooligans* ran for three years in *The Daily Texan*. He is the author of *Rebel Without a Crew: Or How a 23-Year-Old Filmmaker with $7000 Became a Hollywood Player*, now in its third hardback printing. He also is the music mixer on all his films and owns his own record label, Los Hooligans Records. The third eldest of ten children, Robert is a loving brother who is sponsoring his siblings' college tuition. He and wife Elizabeth Avellan are the proud parents of son Rocket Valentino Avellan Rodriguez. Not bad for a guy who was initially turned down by the University of Texas' film school.

Darrell Royal

Darrell Royal is the winningest coach ever to steer a Texas football team. And he did it without God's help. Or at least he didn't ask for His help in pregame prayers. When asked if he prays for victory, Coach, with his down-to-earth sensibility, simply says, "I think the Lord is neutral about these things."

Well, the Lord may not be obsessed with football, but the rest of Texas is, and Darrell gave them what they wanted. During his tenure at the University of Texas, his teams won three national championships, eleven Southwest Conference titles, sixteen bowl appearances, and never had a losing season in twenty-three years. Darrell did it all with integrity, championing high academic standards that have made his players exceptionally successful, on and off the field.

Dewberry Cobbler

Darrell's wife, Edith, prepares this wonderful cobbler for him. As the saying goes, "Behind every great coach lies a great cook."

- 2 cups dewberries (or any other berry), cleaned
- juice of ½ lemon
- 3 tablespoons butter, softened
- 1¾ cups granulated sugar, divided
- ½ cup milk
- 1 cup all-purpose flour
- 1 teaspoon baking powder
- ½ teaspoon salt, divided equally
- 1 tablespoon cornstarch
- 1 cup boiling water

Preheat oven to 375°. Grease an 8-inch square baking pan.

Spread dewberries evenly in pan. Sprinkle lemon juice over berries.

In a small mixing bowl, cream butter and ¾ cup sugar. Stir in milk, flour, baking powder, and half of the salt. Mix until well combined. Drop batter by spoonfuls over berries, covering them evenly.

In a small mixing bowl, mix 1 cup sugar, remaining salt, and cornstarch. Sprinkle this mixture evenly over batter. Gently pour the boiling water over top of all.

Bake for 45 minutes, or until the topping is light brown. Serves 4–6

Ruby's BBQ

Kate's Grilled Rack of Lamb

We often grill outside in the early evenings at our home since we are busy at the restaurant all afternoon. We want something delicious, yet fast. This is a favorite recipe of ours. There are many flavors of Dijon mustard now available. Feel free to try and mix different kinds. Our favorites are Champagne, Provence herbs, horseradish, tarragon, and the coarse style. —Patricia Mares and Luke Zimmerman

1	rack of lamb
5	tablespoons Dijon mustard
2	tablespoons olive oil
1	tablespoon minced garlic
1–2	teaspoons minced anchovy
1–2	tablespoons fresh rosemary, finely chopped
	salt and pepper to taste

Carve the rack into chops by holding the small bone end of the rack and slicing between each bone. (Or have your butcher slice them for you.)

Whisk the mustard and olive oil together in a small bowl. Stir in garlic, anchovy, rosemary, and salt and pepper.

Brush the mixture over the chops, coating the meat well. Marinate chops for 20–30 minutes while you start the grill. When the coals are ready, grill chops, 3–5 minutes per side, until medium rare. Serves 2–3

Ruby's BBQ is an imaginative combination of back-road barbecue joint and worldly jazz and blues cafe. Located on the north end of the University's Drag, Ruby's is one of only a handful of barbecue restaurants nationwide that serve steroid-free, range-fed beef. Charlie Parker's music wafts through the southwestern-style interior along with the indescribably delicious smell of grilling brisket, sausage, chicken, and other goodies cooked in the open brick pit. Ruby's has been a labor of love for owners Patricia Mares and Luke Zimmerman, who opened the restaurant more than a decade ago.

Ben Sargent

Ben Sargent was destined to be a newsman. A sixth-generation Texan, Ben was born in Amarillo into a newspaper family and learned the printing trade when he was twelve. When he was fourteen, he started working for the local daily as a proof runner. Later, he received a degree in journalism from the University of Texas and became a newspaper reporter. But in 1974, Ben entered a different news dimension when he started drawing editorial cartoons for The Austin American-Statesman and the Universal Press Syndicate. Ben has won many national awards, including the Mencken Award and Cox Newspapers' Best of Cox Award. But winning the 1982 Pulitzer Prize distinguished Ben among the best editorial cartoonist in the country. Ben is married to television critic Diane Holloway; they have two children, Elizabeth and Sam.

Pollo y Arroz Texas Style

A traditional New Mexico recipe. Serve it with some tortillas and sliced tomatoes with basil and you've got a meal. —Ben Sargent

3	pounds chicken pieces (use the parts you like best)
	salt and pepper to taste
¼	cup olive oil
1	onion, chopped
1	garlic clove, minced
3	cups canned whole tomatoes with liquid (a little less than a 28-ounce can)
2	teaspoons salt
½	teaspoon oregano
12	black olives, sliced
1	bay leaf
1	tablespoon chili powder
2	cups water
1	cup white rice
1	10-ounce package frozen peas

Season chicken with salt and pepper and brown in olive oil over medium heat in an extra large, heavy frying pan, about 10 minutes. Be careful not to burn chicken. Remove and set aside.

Sauté onion and garlic in the same pan until soft, 5–10 minutes. Stir in tomatoes, salt, oregano, olives, bay leaf, chili powder, and water. Mix well and bring to a boil.

Add chicken and rice. Stir well. Cover tightly, reduce heat to low, and simmer for 25 minutes. Add peas and simmer, covered, for another 5 minutes. Serves 6–8

Joe Sears

Pearl's Molasses Snaps

This is one of my own. In a family of good cooks it's nice to be recognized as the final word on old-fashioned cookies. —Joe Sears

- 2½ cups all-purpose flour
- 1 teaspoon baking powder
- 1½ teaspoons powdered ginger
- 2 teaspoon baking soda
- 1 teaspoon salt
- 1 cup molasses
- ½ cup butter

Preheat oven to 350°.

In a large mixing bowl, sift flour, baking powder, ginger, baking soda, and salt together.

In a small saucepan, heat the molasses, and the butter over medium-low heat, stirring frequently to prevent the mixture from boiling. Set aside to cool.

Stir the molasses mixture into the flour mixture, until smooth. Chill dough for a couple of hours. Roll chilled dough very thin on a lightly floured board. Cut out cookies with a floured cutter. Place on a greased cookie sheet and bake for 10 minutes.

Remove from sheet while still warm, cool in a single layer on a wire rack, and store in a stone jar. Makes about 3½ dozen cookies

As a young boy in rural Oklahoma, writer Joe Sears quietly observed the women folk in his family gossiping and laughing together while they prepared dinners. Those memories of family gatherings forged the core of the characterizations in his plays. His Aunt Pearl Burras, with her generous bosom and deadpan humor, is so believable it's easy to forget there's more than a petticoat under the frock. Aunt Pearl and a host of other characters spin their purely Texan tales in the long-running hit play *Greater Tuna*, which was written by Joe and fellow Austinites Jaston Williams and Ed Howard. It has played all over the world, including the White House, and its sequel, *A Tuna Christmas*, wowed Broadway audiences. Joe and Jaston pack the Paramount Theater whenever they appear there.

For more than sixty years, Beverly Sheffield has worked to keep Austin's "Great Outdoors" close to its people. In 1934, Beverly started his career as playground-activity leader, and over the years moved up to become director of the Austin Parks and Recreation Department. He is credited with guiding the development of the Austin Nature Center, Zilker Botanical Gardens, and the Town Lake area, among many other projects. He retired in 1978, but has remained a tireless volunteer for the community. An octogenarian, Beverly remains sinewy and energetic. He swims regularly—as he has for more than thirty years—at Barton Springs.

Beverly Sheffield

Beat the Heat Eat Dessert

2 quarts (½ gallon) nonfat frozen yogurt
1 12-ounce can frozen lemonade
1 12-ounce carton of Cool Whip, or 1½ cups whipped cream

Let frozen yogurt and lemonade sit at room temperature until soft. In a large mixing bowl, combine frozen yogurt, Cool Whip or whipped cream, and lemonade. Pour into a plastic container, cover, and freeze.

Let soften slightly before serving. Serves 8–12

Jane Sibley

Tequila Lemon Pie

Like your favorite dress, this dessert is simple, elegant, and intriguing. Fit for the most sophisticated gathering or an intimate dinner.

Crust:
- 24 graham crackers, finely crushed
- ¼ cup butter, melted
- ¼ cup brown sugar

Filling:
- ½ cup lemon juice
- 1 14-ounce can sweetened condensed milk
- 3 eggs, beaten
- 3 ounces (6 tablespoons) tequila

Topping:
- 8 ounces sour cream
- 1 tablespoon granulated sugar

To prepare the crust: Mix crushed graham crackers with melted butter and sugar. Press into an 8-inch pie pan to form the crust.

To prepare the filling: In a medium-sized bowl, whisk the eggs and sweetened condensed milk together. Stir in lemon juice and tequila. Pour into a heavy saucepan, and, stirring constantly, slowly bring mixture just to a boil. Remove from heat and let cool slightly. Pour mixture into pie shell.

In a small bowl, whisk together sour cream and sugar. Spoon sour cream over pie filling and refrigerate pie for at least one hour. Makes 1 pie

In 1970, Jane Sibley cast what would most likely become the most important vote in her long reign as an Austin Symphony Orchestra board member. When the future of the symphony was in doubt, Jane was the first to vote against dissolving the orchestra. Jane helped assure the future of the symphony when she and Peggy Brown joined efforts to develop Symphony Square from a complex of four, 100-year-old limestone buildings. The Square houses an amphitheater and the Symphony offices. It is home to summer children's programs and a summer music festival. Jane currently serves as president of the Austin Symphony Orchestra. With her familiar buzzard feather hair dressing, Jane is the perfect ambassador for the arts—elegant, natural and intelligent.

Sincola

Anyone who has seen Sincola perform knows that Austin's premiere pop-punk band has a major label and major success in its future. Signed with the New York-based indie label Caroline Records—the label that produced Smashing Pumpkins and Hole—Sincola has already released two albums. The band's sound "teeters between divine chaos and sublime pop perfection," says the *Austin Chronicle*. Critics also rave about the band's "bona fide star charisma"—from laid-back bassist Chepo Peña, to explosive drummer Terri Lord, to band originators and guitarists Wendel Stivers and Kris Patterson, and the compelling performances of vocalist Rebecca Cannon. A continued rise to national fame seems destined, but Cannon says there will be no Faustian deals. "I want to do well," she says, "but I don't want it to be evil."

Sinful Texas Tacos

1	large onion, diced
1	poblano pepper, chopped
4	garlic cloves, minced
10	mushrooms, sliced
¼	head purple cabbage, chopped
2	tablespoons vegetable oil
½	pound firm tofu
	salt and pepper
2	tablespoons chili powder
½	tablespoon ground cumin
1	medium-sized carrot, grated
2	avocados, cut into slices
	tortillas, warmed
	favorite salsa

Sauté onion, poblano pepper, garlic, mushrooms, and purple cabbage in oil in large skillet over medium heat until vegetables are slightly cooked but still crispy.
Call band members and remind them about band practice.
In a medium mixing bowl, mash tofu with a fork. Season with salt and pepper.
Remember that you left your guitar at last night's show.... Call club and pray.
Throw tofu in with sautéed vegetables. Add chili powder and cumin and cook over low heat for about 5 more minutes.
Finally reach the club, guitar is there!
Fill warm tortilla with tofu-veggie mixture. Top with grated carrot, avocado slices and your favorite salsa. Serves 2–4
Call band members and cancel practice.

Julie Speed

Speedy Pasta e Fagioli

- 1 pound dry pasta (rotini, rotelli, farfalle, or penne)
  olive oil
  a truckload of fresh garlic, minced
- 2 heads escarole, rinsed, drained, and chopped
  (1 pound spinach can be substituted)
- 2 15-ounce cans Progresso cannellini beans with liquid
  paprika (tons)
  red pepper flakes (lots)
  salt and pepper to taste
  Romano cheese, grated (mountains)

Cook pasta al dente according to directions on package and drain.

Cover bottom of a large soup pot with olive oil and sauté garlic over medium-low heat until golden. Throw in the escarole. Stir until the greens are slightly wilted. Add beans, paprika, red pepper flakes, and salt and pepper.

Bring mixture to boil, lower heat to simmer. Add the drained pasta. Heat through and serve with grated Romano cheese on top and with a glass of cheap red wine.

Julie Speed was born in Chicago in 1951 and moved every couple of years after that until she found Austin in 1978. She has called Austin home ever since. A mostly self-taught painter, she has shown in Seattle, Chicago, New York, Los Angeles, Dallas, and San Antonio. Her paintings are very detailed oils, mostly of human figures and faces, that could fit as easily in the 17th century as this one, except for the bizarre twists she adds to each painting, like a fiery halo or a bishop's armless hand floating in mid-air. She is currently being represented by Austin's Tarrytown Gallery, Houston's McMurtrey Gallery, and Santa Fe's Allen La Pides Gallery.

Jill Sterkel

In 1976, Jill Sterkel captured the hearts of Americans by claiming her first Olympic gold medal in swimming when she was only fifteen years old. Her second gold came eight years later, at the 1984 Games, four years after the United States boycotted the 1980 Olympics held in the Soviet Union. And she capped off an incredible Olympic career by winning two bronze medals in 1988. While swimming for the University of Texas, Jill led the Longhorns to national titles in 1981 and 1982, and won sixteen individual national titles. As head coach for the University of Texas' swimming and diving squad, Jill now competes with the same intensity as when she was in the pool. Only now she does it from the sidelines. In her three years as head coach, the Longhorns have finished among the top three in the nation every year.

Roadhouse Pizza

Coach Jill Sterkel has taken the best a roadhouse has to offer—barbecue—and incorporated it into pizza. If you are in a rush, you may use prepared or boxed pizza dough.

Crust:
- 1 tablespoon (1 package) active dry yeast
- 1 cup warm water
- 1 tablespoon sugar
- 2½ cups all-purpose flour

Topping:
- 3 cups KC Masterpiece barbecue sauce
- 3 cups grated mozzarella cheese
- 2 cups chopped fresh mushrooms
- 1½ cups chopped fresh spinach
- 2 cups barbecued chicken, shredded

To prepare the crust: In a large bowl, dissolve the yeast in the warm water. Stir in the sugar. Let sit for 5 minutes. Gradually, add the flour, and work the ingredients together until the dough holds its shape. You may need to add more flour. Turn the dough onto a lightly floured surface, and knead until smooth and elastic. Place the dough in a lightly oiled bowl, cover, and place in a warm place for 1 hour. The dough should double in size.

Preheat the oven to 500°. Divide the dough into 2 portions. Roll the dough out on a floured, flat surface. Form into a 12-inch circle. Place the dough on a baking sheet, pizza pan, or pizza stone. Repeat. Coat each crust with half of the barbecue sauce. Sprinkle half the mozzarella cheese over the sauce. Layer each pizza with half the mushrooms, spinach, and chicken. Bake for 15–20 minutes, until cheese is melted. Makes 2 pizzas

Jim Talbot

Pasta Talbot

This is an easy-to-prepare, healthy, yet vibrantly tasty pasta dish. It's wonderful for summer's dog days because the tomato sauce is not heated. The hot pasta melts the cheese and slightly cooks the tomato sauce without sacrificing the produce's fresh taste.

- 4 cups ripe Roma tomatoes, chopped
- 6 fresh basil leaves
- ½ cup red bell pepper, chopped
- 2 large garlic cloves, minced
- 1 tablespoon olive oil
- 1 pound dry pasta
- 6 ounces mozzarella cheese, shredded
- Parmesan cheese, grated

Set aside 1 cup chopped tomatoes and 2 basil leaves, chopped into thin stripes.

In a blender or food processor, purée remaining tomatoes and basil, bell pepper, garlic, and olive oil.

Meanwhile, cook pasta until al dente, according to directions. Drain and place in a heated pasta bowl. Immediately add mozzarella cheese, puréed tomato mixture, and reserved chopped tomatoes and basil.

Toss and top with grated Parmesan. Serve immediately.

Serves 4–6

It's musicians like Jim Talbot, who play their hearts out in small unassuming clubs, that make Austin a most interesting place to live. They also strengthen the city's claim as the live music capitol of the world. A tall, thin man in his mid-thirties, Jim plays *for* the crowd not *at* the crowd. He plays the blues because he loves to and he lives to play. His brand of old and mainstream blues is creative and spontaneous enough to capture the attention of a bar crowd into the wee hours of the morning.

Travis County Farmers' Market

Twice named one of the "10 best farmers' markets in America," the Travis County Farmers' Market offers peaches, tomatoes, strawberries, corn, watermelon, and the usual harvested items from farms across the state. The market, a former maintenance yard located at 6701 Burnet Road, is more than a quick stop for produce. You'll find fresh baked bread, sausage wraps, goat cheese, fruit salsas, antiques, herbs, and more. As market master C. Hill Rylander says, "We wanted to create a true taste of Texas here, from tomatoes to enchiladas to Texas furnishings. We've got something for the entire family here."

Award Winning Texas Sweet Peach Cobbler

- ¾ cup flour
- pinch salt
- 1 teaspoon baking powder
- 1¼ cups granulated sugar
- 1 teaspoon cinnamon
- ¾ cup whole milk
- ½ cup butter, melted
- 3 cups Texas sweet peaches, peeled and sliced
- ¼ cup granulated sugar
- ½ teaspoon cinnamon

Preheat oven to 350°.

Sift flour, salt and baking powder together in a medium bowl. Add sugar and cinnamon. Slowly add milk, and stir until just mixed.

Pour melted butter into a 9-inch square baking pan. Pour the batter over the butter. Do not stir. Place the peaches on top of the batter. Mix remaining sugar and cinnamon and sprinkle over peaches. Bake for 60 minutes. Serves 6–8.

John Travolta

Phenomenal Grilled Polenta and Wild Mushroom Napoleon

John may be the busiest actor in Hollywood, but he took time to send one of his favorite recipes with a note apologizing for being late.

Polenta:
- 1 tablespoon unsalted butter
- 2 tablespoons finely chopped shallots
- 2½ cups heavy cream
- 2½ cups chicken stock
- ⅛ teaspoon grated nutmeg
- 1½ tablespoons Kosher salt, or to taste
- 1½ cups high-quality cornmeal (not instant polenta)

Mushroom filling:
- 2 tablespoons finely chopped shallots
- 1 tablespoon unsalted butter
- 2 cups sliced cremini mushrooms
- 1 cup sliced shitake mushrooms
- ¼ cup dry white wine
- ¼ cup finely chopped Italian parsley
- salt and pepper to taste
- ½ cups farmer's cheese, shredded
- ½ cup Italian Fontina cheese, shredded
- melted butter

To prepare the polenta: In a 2-quart saucepan, quickly sauté the butter and shallots over medium-high heat until soft. Pour in the cream and chicken stock and bring to boil. Turn down heat and simmer for 5 minutes, stirring frequently. Add nutmeg and salt. Gradually sprinkle the cornmeal into the cream mixture, stirring constantly, until all the cornmeal is added. Continue stirring over medium heat until the polenta becomes thick and creamy and most of the liquid is absorbed. Taste, and add salt and pepper as needed.

It's only fitting that during his great comeback, John Travolta would return to Texas—location of *Urban Cowboy*—to film *Michael*. Austin holds a special place in the heart of the man who captivated a disco-crazy nation in *Saturday Night Fever*, and all but disappeared in the '80s and much of the '90s until *Pulp Fiction*. Now he is commanding a $20 million salary per film and has starred in a string of recent box office hits, including *Get Shorty, Broken Arrow*, and *Phenomenon*. While his salary has skyrocketed, John remains the same caring and kind person he has always been. (Witness his contribution to this cause.) Dancing keeps him toned and youthful even though he admits to an absolute love of food and cooking.

Carefully spread the polenta with a buttered spatula evenly into a buttered baking pan. Set aside until cool, then cover with plastic wrap and put in the refrigerator to set.

To prepare the mushroom filling: In a medium skillet, sauté the shallots and butter over medium heat until soft. Turn the heat to high, add the mushrooms and stir. When the mushrooms begin to dry, add the wine and continue to cook until all the wine has evaporated. Stir and cook for 5 more minutes. Add parsley, and salt and pepper to taste. Remove from the heat and place mixture into a large bowl. Stir in the cheeses. Taste and season again with salt and pepper, if needed.

To assemble: Preheat oven to 400°. Remove the polenta from the fridge and cut into 2-inch squares. Carefully, with a sharp knife, slice the squares in half, making two thin squares instead of one thick one. Place one of the squares on a baking sheet that has been lined with parchment paper. Top the polenta square with the mushroom mixture. Place the other half of the polenta square over the mushroom filling, making a polenta sandwich. Lightly brush the sandwich with butter. Repeat. Bake for about 8 minutes. Serves 8

Rick Trevino

Doctor Time's Cheese Enchiladas

Enchilada sauce:
- 1 tablespoon vegetable oil
- ½ cup flour
- 1 28-ounce can tomato sauce
- 1 teaspoon ground cumin
- 1 teaspoon garlic powder
- 2 tablespoons chili powder
- 2 cups water, or more

- 1½ pounds Colby Longhorn cheese, shredded
- 1 onion, finely chopped
- ½ cups hot cooking oil
- 24 corn tortillas

Preheat oven to 350°.

To prepare the sauce: In a large skillet, heat oil over medium heat and slowly add flour, stirring constantly until flour begins to brown. Add all other sauce ingredients, and simmer, stirring frequently. Add enough water to sauce until it has a gravy-like consistency. Set aside.

Mix Colby cheese and onion together in a medium bowl.

To assemble enchiladas: In a heavy skillet, heat oil until a piece of tortilla sizzles when dropped into it. Dip tortillas, one at a time, in hot oil, and fry briefly. Tortillas should remain soft. Now dip tortilla in enchilada sauce. Fill with cheese and onion mixture. Roll and place, seam down, in an oblong baking pan. Repeat process with the rest of the tortillas, packing enchiladas tightly in the pan. Pour remaining sauce and sprinkle remaining cheese over tortillas. Cover pan with aluminum foil.

Bake enchiladas for about 20 minutes, or until cheese is bubbling. Serve with beans, rice, and salad. Serves 6–8

Señor McGuire

As a child growing up in Austin, Rick Trevino listened to his father's Tejano group, studied classical music, played piano and clarinet, and dreamed of playing baseball. Once out of high school, Rick landed an athletic scholarship to Memphis State University. But luckily for his fans, he turned down second base for the recording studio. Though only in his early twenties, Rick has already made country music history. His first single, *Just Enough Rope*, was the first traditional country single to be released in both English and Spanish versions. Two other singles, *She Can't Say I Didn't Cry* and *Doctor Time*, distinguished Rick as the youngest singer to break the Top 10 the year they were released. Rick has been exposed to the harsh glare of celebrity, but he remains focused. "I really welcomed the role model status, because being able to influence younger kids is what it's all about," he says.

Charles Trois

Born and raised in Philadelphia, Charles Trois followed his heart on a journey that winded across the country and through several careers to Johnson City, Texas. In the late 1950s, Charles played guitar and performed with dozens of local bands before finding success as a guitarist and vocalist with the group Soul Survivor, whose best-known hit was *Expressway to Your Heart*. Charles quit performing in 1969 because he yearned to use his visual art talents, and decided to build an art center in Vermont. He eventually settled in Austin, and, in 1994, opened the Johnson City Feed Mill—a collection of retail shops, restaurants, and a winery—in a refurbished 19th century feed mill and cotton gin.

Très Trois Tuna Spaghetti

The taste is not at all what one would perceive, it's to die for! —Charles Trois

- 2 large cloves garlic, minced
- 4 tablespoons olive oil
- ½ medium onion, diced
- 2 6-ounce cans tuna, drained
- salt and pepper to taste
- ⅛ teaspoon cayenne pepper
- pinch oregano
- 6 large fresh tomatoes, chopped
- 5 fresh basil leaves, chopped
- 1 pound angel hair pasta
- Parmesan cheese, freshly grated

In a large skillet, sauté garlic in oil lightly over medium heat. Add onion, and sauté until limp. Add tuna and seasonings. Stir, being careful to keep tuna in large chunks, and sauté for another 3–5 minutes. Add tomatoes and basil, stir well, and simmer, covered, for 5 minutes over medium-low heat.

Meanwhile, cook pasta according to directions. Drain. Place pasta in preheated ceramic bowl.

Pour sauce over angel hair pasta and serve immediately with grated Parmesan cheese. Serves 6

Tommy Tune

Papa Tune's Red Eye Gravy

- 1 slice Tennessee ham, ¼ inch thick
- flour
- 1 cup beef stock
- ¼ cup Bourbon
- dash hot sauce
- pinch brown sugar
- bay leaf
- salt and pepper

In an iron skillet, cook ham over medium heat until edges are brown, about 3 minutes per side. Remove the ham from the skillet, and add enough flour to the remaining grease to make a roux. Stir over medium heat until flour has browned slightly. Stir in beef stock, bourbon, salt and pepper, hot sauce, brown sugar, and a bay leaf. Simmer over low heat for 5–10 minutes and serve over ham and mashed potatoes or biscuits. YUMMMM. Serves 1–2

Truly a long tall Texan, Tommy Tune may be the most successful choreographer-director in American musical theater. Tommy, who stands six feet six inches tall, certainly is one of Broadway's most recognizable figures. In high school in Houston, the coaches begged him to join the basketball team. But, theater was his dream and after majoring in drama at the University of Texas at Austin, Tommy moved to New York. He has become a fixture there, winning nine Tony Awards and numerous other honors. Tommy has shied away from Hollywood, appearing in only two films, *Hello Dolly!* and *The Boyfriend*, early in his career. Tommy is known for his calm and kind nature in a business known for shouting, hot-tempered men.

Merlin D. Tuttle, Bat Conservation International

Merlin Tuttle has been called the "Indiana Jones of field biologists," but not because his adventures involve discovering football-sized gems or saving lovely ladies in danger. The similarities start with harrowing excursions into dark and gloomy caves, but end with Merlin's worldwide efforts to save the bat from extinction. At home in Austin, Merlin is founder and executive director of Bat Conservation International and protector of the Congress Avenue Bridge bat colony, the largest urban bat populace in the world. More than a million Mexican free-tailed bats spend their summers beneath the downtown Austin bridge. They emerge from the bridge around dusk to feed on anywhere from 10,000 to 30,000 pounds of insects a night.

Merlin Tuttle

Congress Avenue Spicy Shrimp

Pass warm, moist towels to guests and family after they've wolfed down these buttery delicacies.

4	dozen (approximately 2 pounds) large shrimp with shells
2	teaspoons black pepper
1	teaspoon salt
1	teaspoon crushed red pepper
1	teaspoon dried thyme leaves
1	teaspoon dried oregano
1	cup butter
3	teaspoons minced garlic cloves
2	teaspoons Worcestershire sauce
½	cup beer, at room temperature

Wash shrimp in cold water and drain.
Combine all the seasonings and set aside.
Melt the butter in an extra large skillet and add garlic. Sauté until golden. Add the Worcestershire sauce and beer. Turn the heat to high, and add the seasonings. Add the shrimp, and cook for 5–6 minutes, stirring the shrimp so that each one turns pink and is cooked through.
Serve shrimp immediately with finger bowls, large cloth napkins, and a large bowl to collect shells. Serves 4

Jimmie Vaughan

Family Style Hot Spaghetti

This is a great recipe for real people. People who have a life. People who do not have a lot of time but still like good food. Keep the ingredients on hand for a standby meal that always tastes extraordinary.

- 3 tablespoons olive oil
- 3–6 garlic cloves, minced
- 6–8 medium tomatoes, chopped
- 1 tomato bouillon cube
- 1 jalapeño pepper, finely chopped
- Parmesan cheese, grated
- ½ pound dry pasta: spaghetti, fettuccine, or angel hair

Heat large pot of water and cook pasta according to directions.

Meanwhile, heat olive oil in a skillet over medium-low heat. Sauté garlic until golden brown. Add tomatoes, smashing them into oil and garlic. Add tomato bouillon and jalapeño pepper (add more jalapeño pepper, if a spicier flavor is desired). Simmer on low heat for 15 minutes.

Serve over hot pasta with freshly grated Parmesan cheese. Serves 4

A native of Dallas and a long-time resident of Austin, Jimmie Vaughan was a founding member of The Fabulous Thunderbirds. Jimmy enjoyed a six-year, five-album run with the T-Birds. In 1990, he and younger brother Stevie Ray Vaughan completed their first studio collaboration, *Family Style*. Only a few weeks prior to its release, Stevie Ray died in a Wisconsin helicopter crash at the age of thirty-five. His death devastated Jimmie, who lost the desire to perform. He didn't go back on stage until almost three years later when Eric Clapton asked him to open a series of concerts in London. "I just didn't have the guts to tell him no. So I went and got me a band... and went over and did those dates." Vaughan came back from the tour revitalized and that renewed energy was poured into his first solo album, *Strange Pleasure*.

Barry Waite

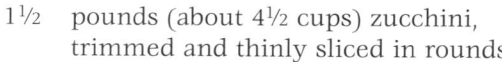

A man often seen running through Austin's many parks helps run one of the city's most important companies. Barry Waite is the senior vice president and general manager of Motorola's Microprocessor and Memory Technologies Group headquartered in Austin. With two state-of-the-art campuses and more than 11,500 employees, Austin is a global focal point for Motorola. The Motorola Foundation provides funding for the Austin Independent School District, the League of Women Voters, and the Center for Battered Women, among other worthy causes. And Austin's Motorolans (Motorola employees) volunteer hundreds of hours each year for non-profit organizations. Barry has worked for Motorola since 1982 at various assignments all over the world, including Scotland and Switzerland. He follows soccer and rugby in the world arena and enjoys jogging.

Motorolan Moussaka

1½	pounds (about 4½ cups) zucchini, trimmed and thinly sliced in rounds
2	tablespoons olive oil
1	large onion, finely chopped
2	green bell peppers, finely chopped
1	garlic clove, peeled and crushed
2	large tomatoes (about 1 pound), chopped
1	tablespoon tomato puree
1	tablespoon chopped fresh mint
	salt and pepper to taste
½	cup (about 4 ounces) thinly sliced Swiss cheese
2	tablespoons all-purpose flour
1¼	cups (10 ounces) plain lowfat yogurt
1	cup (about 3 ounces) lowfat shredded Cheddar cheese

Preheat oven to 400°.

In a large non-stick skillet, brown zucchini, a few at a time, in the olive oil. Remove and set aside.

In the same skillet, sauté the onion, pepper, and garlic over medium heat for about 4 minutes, stirring once or twice. Add a little more oil if necessary. Stir in the tomatoes, tomato puree, mint, salt and pepper and cook for 2 more minutes.

Lightly oil a casserole or baking dish with olive oil. Place half the zucchini in the casserole or baking dish. Cover this layer with half the tomato mixture, and the Swiss cheese. Cover this with the rest of the tomato mixture, and the rest of the zucchini. (At this point, the dish can be stored in a refrigerator for up to 24 hours before being cooked.)

Mix together the flour, yogurt, grated Cheddar cheese, and additional salt and pepper. Pour evenly over the zucchini. Bake for 25 minutes, or until the top is a deep brown. Serves 6

Jerry Jeff Walker

King Ranch Chicken

At only 400 calories per serving and 14 grams fat, this spicy chicken dish can liven up any culinary regimen.

Sauce:
- 2 shallots, minced
- 1 garlic clove, minced
- ¼ cup dry white wine or vermouth
- 1 tablespoon finely diced carrot
- 1 tablespoon finely diced celery
- 1 tablespoon finely diced red bell pepper
- 1 14½-ounce can chicken broth
- 4 tablespoons all-purpose flour
- 1 cup skim milk
- 1 teaspoon salt
- ¼ teaspoon white pepper
- 2 jalapeño chiles, seeded and minced
- 4 tablespoons nonfat cream cheese

- 1 large diced onion
- ½ cup each diced red and yellow bell peppers
- ½ cup diced green chiles
- 12 corn tortillas, quartered and toasted
- butter-flavored vegetable spray
- salt and pepper, to taste
- 8 chicken breasts, boned, skinned, and cut in cubes
- 1 teaspoon chili powder
- ¾ cup lowfat Monterey Jack cheese, shredded
- ½ cup green chiles
- 1 tomato, diced

In the early 1960s when he was still a teen, Jerry Jeff Walker blew out of Oneonta, New York, with a Stella guitar on his back, and a tattered copy of Dylan Thomas' book on Welsh mysticism in his hip pocket. A decade later, after producing several hits and writing the classic *Mr. Bojangles*, he landed in Austin. There, he found a creative community that accepted his mix of folk, rock, country and anything else. Jerry became one of the arbiters of the Austin-based Texas music boom. Jerry Jeff's Birthday Weekend, which he throws for himself every year in Austin, has become a fixture on the calendars of his fans across the country. He is married to Susan—the object of his affections, the mother of their two children, and his manager.

Preheat oven to 350°.

To prepare sauce: In a medium saucepan, bring shallots, garlic, white wine, carrot, celery, bell pepper, and chicken broth to a boil. Lower heat to simmer. In a small mixing bowl, place flour and gradually pour in the milk, stirring to dissolve flour completely. Pour the milk mixture slowly into the hot chicken broth, stirring constantly. Simmer the sauce over medium-low heat, stirring frequently, until thickened. Add salt, white pepper, jalapeño chiles, and cream cheese. Stir until the cheese is melted. Set sauce aside.

Coat a medium skillet with vegetable spray and sauté the onion, bell peppers, and chiles over medium heat until softened. Season with salt and pepper and set aside.

Spray the tortillas lightly with a buttered-flavored vegetable spray on both sides and place on cookie sheets. Toast in preheated oven for 8 minutes. Tortillas will not be crisp. Cut into quarters.

To assemble: Place half the tortillas in a 13x9-inch casserole. Place half the chicken on top of the tortillas and season with salt, pepper and chili powder. Top with half the vegetable mixture. Repeat. Pour the sauce over all. Top with shredded Monterey Jack cheese, diced green chiles and tomatoes. Cover with aluminum foil and bake for 40 minutes, removing the foil the last 10 minutes of baking. Let sit 10 minutes before serving. Serves 8

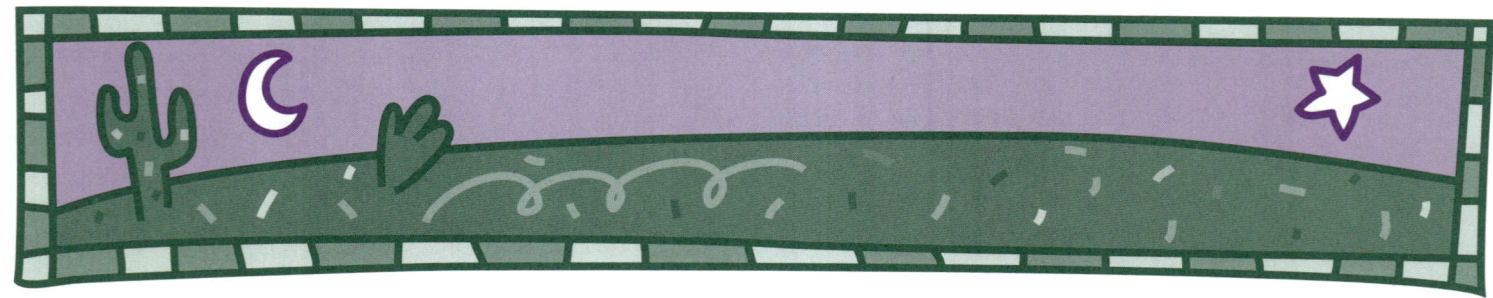

Don Walser

Jailhouse Rolls

These yummy rolls are somewhat like a cross between a brioche, a dinner roll, and a biscuit. They are quick to make, because there is no rising time, and they're real tasty.

This is one of my favorites that my wife used to fix a lot. —Don Walser

- 2 packages (2 tablespoons) dry yeast
- 1½ cups warm water
- 1 cup mashed potatoes
- 1 cup margarine or butter, melted
- 3 eggs, beaten
- 1½ tablespoons salt
- 1 cup granulated sugar
- 7 cups all-purpose flour

Preheat oven to 350°.

In a medium bowl, mix yeast and water. Let stand for 15 minutes. Stir in potatoes, margarine or butter, eggs, salt and sugar. Pour liquid mixture into large bowl containing flour and stir with a wooden spoon until smooth. Mixture will be soft. Drop by spoonfuls onto a greased cookie sheet. Bake for 25–30 minutes, or until rolls are golden. Makes 3 dozen rolls

Note: Dough will keep in the refrigerator for 4 or 5 days and can be used as needed.

Don Walser has been called Texas' answer to Luciano Pavarotti. He and his Pure Texas Band play mostly country classics, and Don's tenor voice is so perfect and clear that it almost defies nature. But full-time singing and performing for a living is something Don has done only since 1988. Don deferred his dream of singing country, while he and his wife, Pat, raised their four children. They also took in several foster children. For forty-five years, Don worked for the National Guard, rising from mechanic, to administrator, to auditor. Now Don is living his dream. He's toured the country with Tish Hinojosa's Border Tour, released several albums, and he's been the star attraction on a Carnival cruise ship. Don has remained true to his music, and his singing has captured the simple essence of country.

Monte Warden

Monte Warden is happiest making music and living in the town he was raised in—Austin. Although he's definitely talented enough to be with a major record label, the Austin native does not like the compromises that come along with the money. So he does it his way. His catchy melodies have been compared to Buddy Holly's tunes. In *Here I Am*, his best album yet, he fuses momentum and hummability in a rock 'n' roll album with a Texas dance-hall twang. *Here I Am* was named one of the five best albums of the year by the 1995-96 Austin Music Awards. Critics anticipate that Monte will succumb to the tug of Nashville, but for now the guitarist is happy with Austin's independent label, Watermelon Records. He gets to make good music, instead of watching the bottom line.

Mima's Chicken Fried Steak

*Mima was my grandmother. To those unfortunate folks who weren't her grandchildren, she was called Anna Carson. Her cookin' was the best I ever tasted. This recipe is based on her C.F.S. recipe. She never made it the same way twice. But she **always** made a great C.F.S. —Monte Warden*

	flour
	cornmeal
	2 paper sacks (one inside the other)
½	teaspoon salt
½	heaping tablespoon black pepper
½	teaspoon poultry seasoning
¼	teaspoon garlic powder
6	Ritz crackers, mashed
2	egg yolks
¼	cup milk
10–16	ounce sirloin patty
1½	cups bacon grease

Place 2 handfuls of flour and 1 handful of cornmeal in the paper sacks. Add salt, pepper, poultry seasoning, garlic powder, and mashed Ritz crackers.

In a small bowl, beat egg yolks and milk. Place meat patty in the bowl, pressing it down to make sure both sides are submerged. Let it soak for a minute or so. Put patty in the paper sack with flour mixture and shake vigorously. Deep fry the patty in bacon grease until golden brown.* Serves 2–4

*Some namby-pamby Yankee carpetbaggers may request that their C.F.S. be cooked medium or medium-rare. Bless their hearts. They just don't know no better.

Sarah Weddington

Fort Smith Apple Pie

This unusual and savory version of America's favorite comes from Sarah's friend Sandy Nichols of Austin. It's an updated version of a very old family recipe. The finished product is a wonder to behold—halved apples swimming in a wonderful gooey syrup. It looks like a fantasy from a master baker's pantry.

Sour cream pastry:
- 2¼ cups all-purpose flour
- 3 tablespoons sour cream
- 1 egg
- ¾ cup frozen butter, cut into small cubes
- ½ teaspoon salt

- 4–6 golden delicious apples
- ½–¾ cup butter, cut into cubes
- 1½ cups sugar
- 1½ cups boiling water

Preheat oven to 450°.

To prepare the pastry: Place ingredients into a food processor and process, turning on and off for 15 seconds. Continue processing until a ball just forms on the blade. Do not over process or the crust will be tough. Form into a flattened ball, wrap in plastic wrap, and refrigerate until firm and ready to roll out.

Use a large oval or rectangular baking dish, preferably at least 2 inches deep, for this recipe. Roll out pastry and line dish with it, making a decorative edge at top. Refrigerate.

Put a tea kettle on to boil with at least 2 cups water. Peel, core, and cut apples in halves. Place flat side down on pastry. Fill in spaces with quartered apples, but try not to use pieces smaller than that. Scatter cubed butter over apples. Combine sugar and boiling water, and pour over apples. (You may vary the amount of sugar used, depending on your taste and the tartness of the apples. Adjust the amount of water used to equal the amount of sugar used.)

Bake for about 15 minutes, then reduce heat to 350°, and continue baking until apples can be pierced easily with a sharp knife and the crust is brown, at least another 30 minutes. Serve warm in bowls, spooning some of the delicious syrup over the apple half and pastry. (*Makes enough to serve seconds!*) Makes 1 pie

In 1973, a 26-year-old rookie lawyer, just five years out of the University of Texas' law school, successfully argued what many consider to be the most important legal benchmark for women in the latter half of this century. *Roe v. Wade* was Sarah Weddington's first contested case, and the favorable ruling made her the youngest woman ever to win a case in the U.S. Supreme Court. Sarah is now a writer, lecturer, and teacher at the University of Texas. She speaks extensively on the development of leadership skills and women's issues, and continues to champion abortion rights and other causes. Sarah is a former Texas state representative and served as an assistant to President Jimmy Carter, directing the administration's work on women's issues.

Steven Weinberg

Steven Weinberg is a world leader in quantum field theory whose discoveries reshaped the way we view the atom, and, for that matter, the universe. His work in physics has been honored with numerous awards, including the 1979 Nobel Prize in physics and the 1991 National Medal of Science. He is author of the prize-winning book *The First Three Minutes: A Modern View of the Origin of the Universe*, *The Discovery of Subatomic Particles*, *Elementary Particles and the Laws of Physics* (with Richard Feynman), and *Dreams of a Final Theory*, among other titles. Steven holds the Josey Regental Chair of Science at the University of Texas, and is a member of the physics and astronomy departments. Before coming to Austin in 1982, he taught at Columbia, Berkeley, M.I.T., and Harvard.

Anhydrous Zucchini

Those who take a morose view of the biological limitations of the human species should consider the zucchini. In countless British and American restaurants, this vegetable (courgettes to native FRSs) is boiled to the point of disintegration, and served in a watery stew of tomatoes and onions. It is natural to conclude that zucchini is an evolutionary dead end, kept under cultivation only by a government subsidy of ill-advised agriculture. Yet zucchini can be quite good to eat, and without excessive trouble. Here is my own recipe.

First, wash your zucchini. I don't know why, but zucchini come rather dirty from the greengrocer. Perhaps grocers can't believe anyone will actually eat zucchini.

Next, slice each zucchini unevenly, the slices averaging 5–10 mm thickness. The point of their being uneven is that then some slices will get cooked more rapidly, and you can eat them while you're cooking the rest.

Then, put some olive oil in the bottom of a skillet, enough to wet the bottom everywhere, and heat it on a high flame for a minute or two. Put the zucchini slices in the oil, and turn them over nervously several times until they begin to brown.

At this point, you can begin to be inventive. Add salt or soy sauce, and also garlic or oregano if you like. As slices become golden brown, remove from the pan and dry on a paper towel. Try not to eat them all before you have a chance to bring them to the table.

Not very long ago, Shannon Wheeler was an out-of-work cartoonist who couldn't *even* get published in the *Austin Chronicle*. Now with the super success of his superhero character, Too Much Coffee Man, Shannon is a celebrity. Shannon's TMCM comics sell across the nation; he has created an animated television commercial starring TMCM for Converse; and he presides over a merchandising gold mine—TMCM coffee cups, T-shirts, and bath sponges. He gets letters from all over the world praising his work. But success has not come without a price for Shannon. He can't get a regular cappuccino anymore, a drawback, for a jittery Shannon who drinks almost as much coffee as his creation. "They insist on making it four times stronger for me."

Wiley Wiggins

Pam Francis Photography

Wiley Wiggins' gentle acerbic manner and lovely, man-in-the-moon face made him the charismatic center of his movie debut in Richard Linklater's *Dazed and Confused*. The then-seventeen-year-old Wiley was hanging outside of Captain Quackenbush's, the granddaddy of Austin coffee shops, when he was discovered. Next came *Love and a .45*, *Boys*, and more fame for Wiley. But Wiley remains centered in Austin, where he is a contributing editor to *FringeWare Review* magazine, makes hip look tragic at alternative bookstores, and runs around barefoot in Austin's many parks. Future plans, well, they are not really plans, but more like a wish list. "I wanna be a cowboy, that's what I wanna be," he says wryly.

Dazed and Confused Lasagna

All of this will be extremely yummy. Trust me. —Wiley Wiggins

2	15-ounce cans black beans
¼	cup veggie broth
1	teaspoon cumin
½	teaspoon salt
10	no-bake lasagna noodles
2	cups ricotta cheese
3	cups shredded Monterey Jack cheese
3	cups (30-ounce jar) spaghetti sauce
5	garlic cloves, minced

Preheat oven to 375°.

Get a lasagna pan. Get a bowl. Drain both cans of beans, and pour beans into a bowl. Mash them with a spoon. Add veggie broth, cumin, and salt. Mix.

Arrange 5 uncooked lasagna noodles at the bottom of the pan. Put half the bean mixture on noodles. Next, spread one cup of the ricotta cheese over the beans, and a cup of the Jack. Pour half the spaghetti sauce over the top. Repeat with another layer of beans, ricotta, Jack, and spaghetti sauce. Top with remaining Jack and minced garlic. Cover with aluminum foil. Bake 30 minutes; remove foil. Bake for 20 minutes more. Let sit for 5 minutes before cutting. Serves 6–8

Van Wilks

Wok 'n' Roll Yardbird Stir Fry

Presentation of the meal is very important. Thought should be applied to audio and video enhancement. Suggested background music might include "Everybody was Kung Fu Fighting," soundtracks from Bruce Lee movies, or my favorite, "The Theme from Kung Fu, the TV series." Just don't substitute David Carradine info-mercials. As Julia Child might or might not say, "The proper background will give an intangible legitimacy to the integrity of the dish."

In the end, stir frying is easy. Even a rock 'n' roll guitar player can present an edible and nutritious dish... Just be sure to seek out "volunteers" for clean up duty! Wok 'n' roll!! — Van Wilks

2	chicken breasts, skinned, boned and thinly sliced
3	tablespoons cornstarch
4	tablespoons soy sauce
1	fresh garlic clove (mash it up)
1	tablespoon ginger, peeled and finely minced
2	tablespoons peanut oil
½	pound fresh broccoli
2	medium onions (Texas 1015s are best), thinly sliced
¼	pound fresh mushrooms, sliced
1	cup chicken broth
2	cups fresh bean sprouts
	cracked black pepper and salt to taste
	cooked rice
	soy sauce
	Chinese chili sauce

Place chicken, cornstarch, soy sauce, garlic, and ginger in a glass bowl; stir until chicken is thoroughly coated. Let it stand for 15 minutes.

Heat oil in wok over high heat. Add chicken and stir fry until browned. Remove chicken to a plate. Stir fry broccoli and onion in wok for 3 minutes. Add mushrooms, and stir fry for 2 more minutes. Return chicken to wok. Pour in chicken broth, lower heat, and cover, simmering gently for about 3–5 minutes or until vegetables are tender but still crisp. Stir in bean sprouts. Season with cracked pepper and salt, to taste. Serve over rice with soy sauce and Chinese chili sauce on the side. Serves 2–4

In Austin, a city known for its great guitarists, Van Wilks has long been lauded as one of the city's master players. In fact, his talent as a guitarist have won him consistent critical praise and a string of honors, including a place in the Texas Music Hall of Fame. He also holds the distinction of being voted the *Austin Chronicle*'s Best Hard Rock Band four years in a row. Van Wilks creates music that brings his blues roots to the contemporary cutting edge with funk, hard rock, and pop flavors. Van and his band have toured the nation with such acts as ZZ Top, Heart, and many others.

Jaston Williams

Vera's Lime Pie

Sometimes the simplest things in life are the best. That's how it is with this dessert—pure lime flavor in a succulent pie.

- ½ cup butter, melted and cooled
- 1 cup granulated sugar
- juice of 4 limes
- 3 eggs, beaten
- 8-inch pie shell, unbaked

Preheat oven to 350°.
In a medium mixing bowl whisk sugar, eggs and lime juice together. Add the melted butter and beat until the mixture is smooth. Pour mixture into the pie shell and bake for 45 minutes, or until the filling turns light brown on top. Let the pie cool and serve with a few drops of lime juice on top of each slice. Make 1 pie

"A big part of our success is that we started in Austin," Jaston Williams once told a *Texas Monthly* reporter. "It's such a great place to create—people are so appreciative." Born in El Paso, Jaston discovered Austin after attending Houston's San Jacinto College and working for San Antonio's now-defunct First Repertory Company. It was in Austin during the '70s that Jaston teamed up with Joe Sears and Ed Howard to write *Greater Tuna*. Since then Jaston and Joe have regularly toured nationwide and won over hundreds of thousands of fans. Jaston is Vera Carp, who is catty and shrill. *Greater Tuna* and its sequel, *A Tuna Christmas*, have earned Jaston a nationwide following and financial freedom. But, home is still Austin. "I love New York, and I can handle L.A., but I don't want to live in either of those places. I'm a Texan forever," says Jaston.

Lucinda Williams

Secret of Longevity Sweet Corn Bread

This recipe was handed down to me by my father, the poet Miller Williams, who got it from his mother, Angie, who lived to be 100. Don't leave off the preheating of the skillet! —Lucinda Williams

- 1 cup finely ground yellow cornmeal
- 1 cup all-purpose flour
- ¼ cup granulated sugar
- 4 teaspoons baking powder
- ½ teaspoon salt
- 1 egg
- 1 cup milk
- 3 tablespoons bacon drippings or vegetable oil
- 1 tablespoon Crisco or vegetable oil

Preheat oven to 425°.

In a large mixing bowl, place the cornmeal, flour, sugar, baking powder, and salt. Mix well.

In a small bowl, beat together the egg and milk and blend in bacon drippings or oil. Gradually, pour liquid ingredients into flour mixture, while stirring. Beat with spoon until mixture is thoroughly blended.

Place shortening or vegetable oil in an 8- or 9-inch cast iron skillet and heat in the preheated oven. When good and hot, pour off excess oil. Pour corn bread mixture into hot skillet and bake for 20–25 minutes. Serves 4

"In her voice we can hear the sound of desire itself," says the *Rolling Stone*. Lucinda Williams can steal your heart away with her soprano twang and perfectly-worded stories. She grew up in Louisiana in a musical household, although as a child she was as interested in the gothic fiction of Flannery O'Connor and Eudora Welty as she was in the music of Robert Johnson and The Doors. At sixteen, she launched her career as a singer and songwriter, singing in coffee houses in her home state. Eventually Lucinda migrated to Austin. Her 1988 composition *Passionate Kisses* became a hit for Mary Chapin Carpenter and went on to earn a Grammy in 1994.

Kim Wilson

Kirk Tuck

Kim Wilson has been around music since his early days growing up in Detroit, but it wasn't until high school that he started to develop a passion for the blues. "I took trombone and guitar lessons, moved to California, and played in high school." In the '70s, Kim traveled to Austin where he met guitarist Jimmie Vaughan. The two formed The Fabulous Thunderbirds and became the house band at Antone's, proving beyond a reasonable doubt that white boys can play the blues. During this time, Kim came under the wing of one of the greatest bluesmen in history, Muddy Waters. Along with the many hits, including *Tuff Enuff* and *Wrap It Up*, recorded by the T-Birds, Kim has made two critically praised solo albums, *Tiger Man* and *That's Life*.

Italian Cream Cake

Cake:
- 1 cup butter
- 2 cups granulated sugar
- 5 egg yolks, beaten
- 2 cups all-purpose flour
- 1 teaspoon baking soda
- 1 cup buttermilk
- 1 teaspoon vanilla extract
- 1¾ cups shredded coconut
- 1 cup chopped pecans
- 5 egg whites, stiffly beaten

Frosting:
- 8 ounces cream cheese, at room temperature
- ¼ cup butter
- 4 cups powdered sugar
- 1 teaspoon vanilla
- 1 cup shredded coconut
- 1 cup chopped pecans

Preheat oven to 350°. Butter and flour 3 round layer cake pans.

In a large mixing bowl, cream the butter and sugar. Stir in beaten egg yolks. Stir the flour and baking soda, alternatively with the buttermilk, into the creamed mixture, mixing well. Stir in the vanilla, coconut, and chopped pecans. Whip egg white to stiff peaks and fold into rest of ingredients. Pour into cake pans. Bake for 30 minutes. Remove from oven and cool on wire racks.

Meanwhile, to prepare the frosting: Beat cream cheese and butter until smooth. Add sugar and mix well. Add vanilla, coconut, and pecans.

Arrange 1 cake layer on a cake plate. Spread with frosting. Set second layer on top and spread with more frosting. Repeat with third layer and then frost sides of cake.
Makes 1 cake

Marion Winik

My Father's Tuna Spread

Great with dad's drink—Absolut vodka, fresh from the freezer. —Marion Winik

1   6-ounce can white tuna, drained
1   9½-ounce Progresso Olive Salad or Progresso Pepper Salad, drained
    A little mayo to taste

Place ingredients in food processor and chop for a few seconds only. Serve as a hors d'oeuvre with crackers or sliced baguette.

Marion Ettlinger

Marion Winik is the author of *Telling: Confessions, Concessions, and Other Flashes of Light*, a collection of brutally honest and humorous stories with titles like WHAT I KNOW ABOUT ABORTION WON'T FIT ON THE HEAD OF A PIN, WOMEN WHO LOVE MEN WHO DON'T PAY THEIR PARKING TICKETS, and SUBURBAN TEENS ON ACID 1972-1975. Raised in Ocean Township, New Jersey, Marion played the role of the rebellious teen. At seventeen, she attended Rhode Island's Brown University and moved to Austin after graduation. After a two-year stint in New York, she returned to Texas with her husband, Tony Heubach. Marion is a regular commentator on National Public Radio's *All Things Considered*.

Bill Wittliff

Connie Todd

Bill Wittliff is a master wordsmith, having crafted engrossing stories nearly his entire life. When he was small, Bill and his family moved to Gregory, Texas, where his mother ran a small telephone office during World War II (these experiences provided the basis for the film *Raggedy Man*). After graduating from the University of Texas, Bill and his wife, Sally, founded a book publishing company, The Encino Press, which specializes in regional material about Texas and the Southwest. Bill is especially skillful at writing for the big screen. His credits include *Honeysuckle Rose, Country, The Cowboy Way,* and *Legends of the Fall*. He was also the author and executive producer of the television adaptation of Larry McMurtry's novel, *Lonesome Dove*. The enduringly popular miniseries won seven Emmys.

Mexican Cabrito Frito

½ pound bacon
1 large Texas sweet onion, diced
4 garlic cloves, minced
2 pounds cabrito, chopped
  (or beef or venison if cabrito is not handy)
  salt, cumin, chili powder to taste
3–4 cups water
1 15-ounce can Wolf Brand Chili (absolutely no beans)
1 15-ounce can yellow or white hominy, drained
1 15-ounce can cream-style corn
8 ounces Cheddar or processed American cheese, cubed
1 bag corn chips
  red chili piquines for garnish
  1 small jicama, diced, for garnish
  1 bunch green onions, tops only, chopped, for garnish

In a large skillet, fry bacon until well done, remove, drain, and crumble. Drain all but 4 tablespoons of the bacon grease from the skillet, and sauté the onion and garlic over medium heat until tender. Add the chopped cabrito, stir well and brown, seasoning to taste with salt, cumin and chili powder. Add water and simmer, uncovered, about 30 minutes over low heat.

Stir in Wolf Brand Chili, hominy, and creamed corn. Heat through. Add cheese and stir until melted. Mix in crumbled bacon.

Spread out large pile of corn chips to cover bottom of serving platter. Pour heated mixture over corn chips. Sprinkle with red chili piquines, jicama, and green onion tops (the colors of the Mexican flag). *Salute and serve immediately. ¡Buen provecho, amigos!* Serves 6–8

Sandy Wood

Stellar Dessert Meringues

These heavenly cookies are as light as the clouds with a rich chocolate kick.

- 2 egg whites
- ⅔ cup granulated sugar
- pinch salt
- 1 cup sweet chocolate chips
- 1 cup chopped nuts: pecans, walnuts, or almonds
- 1 teaspoon vanilla

Preheat oven to 350°.

Beat egg whites in a medium-sized mixing bowl until frothy. Add sugar and salt and continue to beat at high speed until mixture forms stiff peaks. Fold in chips, nuts and vanilla. Drop by spoonfuls on foil-covered baking sheet.

Place in preheated oven. Turn oven off immediately. Leave cookies in oven for at least 3 hours without opening oven door. May be left overnight. Makes 15 large cookies.

Sandy Wood's heavenly voice sets the tone for the award-winning radio series *Star Date*, which airs on public radio stations across the country. The popular radio segment brings the heavens down to earth by making sense of complicated science and by explaining the significance of astronomy in our daily lives. *Star Date* offers information that is both informative and entertaining, including the latest in skywatching, news about space science, and pieces on historical figures and events. In its sixteenth year, the longest running science feature in the country is produced by the University of Texas at Austin's McDonald Observatory.

Charles Alan Wright

Greenbrier Photography

Charles Alan Wright has held many distinguished positions and broken plenty of legal ground throughout his illustrious career. He has argued twelve cases before the U.S. Supreme Court, written fifteen books, received many honors and awards from his peers, and inspired hordes of University of Texas law students. But his aborted role as President Richard Nixon's counsel in the Watergate hearings is the position that has earned Charles the most ink in history books. He quit Nixon mid-hearing, upset that he had not been told about the White House tapes. Charles has been on the UT faculty since 1955, and, currently, holds the William B. Bates Chair for the Administration of Justice. He enjoys reading and reviewing mysteries, fishing, and coaching the Legal Eagles, an intramural touch football team. He is married to Eleanor Custis; they have four children.

Microwave Chocolate Bread Pudding

Oh, the wonders of electromagnetic cooking.... This rich and chocolatey dessert takes only a few minutes to prepare—and will probably take less time for your appreciative family to wolf down.

2	rounded tablespoons semisweet chocolate chips
1/2	cup milk
1	egg, beaten
2	tablespoons granulated sugar
1/4	teaspoon vanilla
2	slices white bread, cubed
1	cup heavy cream, whipped
1	tablespoon granulated sugar
1	teaspoon vanilla

In a 2-cup Pyrex bowl, microwave chocolate and milk at high setting, uncovered, for 60–90 seconds, or until the mixture is steaming hot.

Carefully, remove from microwave and stir until the chocolate dissolves into the milk. Let cool.

Now whisk egg, sugar, and vanilla into the milk mixture. Stir in bread. Return to microwave and cook on medium-high setting (70%), uncovered, for 2 minutes and rotate dish. Cook for another 1–2 minutes until puffed.

Add granulated sugar and vanilla to whipped cream and spoon over pudding. May be served warm or cold. Serves 2

Y.O. Ranch

Bertie's Y.O. Venison

I have known this way of cooking venison since I was very young and have taught many people to cook meat this way. Serve with gravy made from the flour and some of the leftover milk and good hot bread. —Bertie Varner, Y.O. Ranch chef

- 2 pounds venison (may be slices ¼-inch thick, or the small bits you get when trimming out hocks)
- 1 12-ounce can evaporated milk
- salt and pepper to taste
- garlic powder (optional)
- onion powder (optional)
- flour
- vegetable oil

Pound venison flat with meat pounder.

Place venison in a large bowl with evaporated milk and enough water to completely cover the meat. Allow to stand for 1 hour.

Remove meat, a piece at a time, allowing it to drain only slightly. Season with salt and pepper and other seasonings and dredge in flour.

In a heavy skillet, heat about 1½ inches of oil to 375°. Drop floured venison, a few pieces at a time, into hot oil. Fry until golden brown, about 2–3 minutes. Do not overcook or the meat will become dry and tough. Serves 4–6

The Y.O. Ranch lies in the heart of the Texas Hill Country. With 40,000 acres, the 100-year-old ranch is one of Texas' largest working ranches and a destination dude ranch. Today, fourth-generation Gus Schreiner oversees all guest activities. Dudes can drive cattle, hunt, hike nature trails, relax by the pool, try some of the world-famous Y.O. Ranch-style grub, or view some of the 10,000 animals that roam the grounds. The Y.O is the largest exotic wildlife ranch in North America and is famous for its herd of 1,500 Texas longhorns and fifty-five species of animals, including native white-tailed deer and turkeys, as well as giraffe, ostrich, wildebeest, scimitar-horned oryx, addax, European fallow deer, Japanese sika, Iranian red sheep, and zebra.

Ziller House

Dill Crusted Salmon with Corn and Asparagus Relish

2 tablespoons butter
1 tablespoon fresh lemon juice
2 tablespoons extra virgin olive oil
3 tablespoons chopped fresh dill
1 20-ounce salmon fillet, boned

Relish:
2 tablespoons olive oil
2 cups fresh or frozen corn
2 medium-sized bell peppers, one red and one yellow, cored, seeded and finely chopped
1 medium onion, finely chopped
1 cup fresh asparagus tips
2 teaspoons vinegar, preferably balsamic
2 teaspoons chopped fresh thyme, or 1 teaspoon dried thyme
salt and freshly ground black pepper to taste

Preheat oven to 450°.
Melt butter in saucepan or microwave. Blend in lemon juice, olive oil, and dill. Place salmon in baking dish skin side down. Cover evenly with butter mixture. Bake for 10–15 minutes, depending on the thickness of the fillet, basting once or twice with butter mixture. The salmon will be lightly crusted on the outside and moist on the inside. When removing the salmon, slide a spatula between the skin and the flesh of the fish. The skin will adhere to the dish.
While salmon is baking, prepare relish. Heat olive oil in a large skillet over medium heat. Add corn, peppers, and onion. Cook until tender, but still crisp, stirring occasionally. Add asparagus, vinegar, thyme, and salt and pepper. Cook 3–5 minutes more, until vegetables are tender.
Serve salmon on a platter, surrounded by relish. Serves 4

Ziller House could bill itself as the "Bed and Breakfast to the Stars," but it's far too discreet to do anything of the sort. Exactly why this wooded retreat on a rise overlooking the south shore of Town Lake has attracted the likes of Lyle Lovett and Julia Roberts (at the same time), Clint Eastwood, Walter Cronkite, Meg Ryan, and Dennis Quaid. You won't find yourself in chintz hell either, like frilly, formal B&Bs. The Italian-style mansion, built in 1938, offers a unique brand of contemporary sophistication in its architecture, furnishings, and services. Sam Kindred and Wendy Sandberg are Ziller House's unaffected and gracious owners.

Nadya Zybine & Rafael Padilla

Havana Pork Chops

This is a Cuban dish and a favorite of Rafael's. He suggests serving it with black beans and fried platano.

- ¼ cup apple juice
- 3 tablespoons lemon juice
- 1 onion, finely minced
- 1 garlic clove, minced
- 1½ tablespoons chopped fresh savory, or 1 tablespoon dried savory
- salt and pepper to taste
- 4 center cut pork chops
- ¼ cup applesauce
- 1 red apple, sliced ½ inch thick
- 1 tart green apple, slice ½ inch thick

In a large bowl, combine the apple juice, lemon juice, onion, garlic, savory, and salt and pepper. Add the pork chops. Marinate for at least 30 minutes in the refrigerator. Turn occasionally, making sure all sides are coated.

Preheat oven to 350°.

Remove the chops from the marinade and place them on a roasting pan in the preheated oven. Bake for 10 minutes.

Meanwhile, place 3 tablespoons of remaining marinade in a small bowl. Stir in applesauce. Brush the chops with the applesauce mixture and continue baking, brushing frequently, until the chops are done, about 20–30 minutes.

While chops are baking, cook the sliced apples in the remaining marinade in a heavy saucepan. Boil over medium heat until the apples are tender and marinade is cooked thoroughly. Spread a quarter of the marinade mixture on each plate and top with a pork chop. Serves 4

In the marriage of Nadya Zybine and Rafael Padilla, one can find the melding of the great traditions and ballet cultures from around the world. The wife and husband team are principal dancers for Ballet Austin, the city's premier ballet company. Nadya is a third-generation dancer trained by her father, Alex Zybine, who danced with the Ballet Russe de Monte Carlo, and her mother, Violette Zybine, director of the Academia del Ballet Guadalajara. Nadya refined her talents at the Joffrey Ballet in New York. Rafael was born in Havana, Cuba, and joined the Ballet Nacional de Cuba when he was 17. He has worked with such world-famous dancers, teachers, and choreographers, as Rudolf Nureyev, Fernando Alonso, Irina Copakova, and many others.

Index

A

A Cowboy's Favorite Meat Loaf, 6
A Girl's German Potato Salad, 57
A Master's Creamed Corn, 40
A Roper's Breakfast, 83
A Scot's Dutch Witloof by Way of Texas, 91
A Treasure of a Tamale Pie, 93
A Woman on the Verge of Herbed Orzo, 95
After the Gig Migas, 14
Ancho Sauce, Traditional, 63
Anhydrous Zucchini, 136
Appetizers
    LBJ Ranch Spicy Cheddar Wafers, 72
    Marinated Portobello Mushrooms with
        Black Bean Sauce, 46
    My Father's Tuna Spread, 143
Apple Pie, Fort Smith, 135
Apple Pie, Veronique's, 86
Applesauce Cake, Mayberry, 87
Arresting Barbecued Pork Loin Chops, 73
As Promised Texas Pralines, 42
Award Winning Texas Sweet Peach Cobbler, 122

B

Banana Buttermilk Pancakes, Sunday Morning, 19
Banana Pudding, Shade Tree, 47
Barn Dance Potluck Potato Salad, 100
Barton Creek Lobster and Vodka Gazpacho, 17
Basil and Raspberry Shrimp Pasta, Fall Creek, 10
Beans
    Brown Beans by Bullock, 30
    Dazed and Confused Lasagna, 138
    Insalata Pasta e Fagioli, 50
    Marinated Portobello Mushrooms with
        Black Bean Sauce, 46
    Passionate Lentil and Spinach Soup, 18
    Rave LaFave Veggie Chili, 77
    River City Green Bean Rolls, 64
    Shadywood Showdown Chili, 66
    Shannon Wheeler's Bachelor Burritos, 137
    Speedy Pasta e Fagioli, 119
    Texas Chainsaw Chili, 65

Beat the Heat Eat Dessert, 116
Beef
    A Cowboy's Favorite Meat Loaf, 6
    A Treasure of a Tamale Pie, 93
    The Broken Spoke's Chicken Fried Steak with
        Cream Gravy, 27
    Chuy's Tex-Mex Chili Con Carne, 38
    Go to Hell Prime Rib, 89
    James Michener's Beef Bourguignon, 90
    Mima's Chicken Fried Steak, 134
    Shadywood Showdown Chili, 66
    Texas Chainsaw Chili, 65
Bertie's Y.O. Venison, 147
Bevo Tackles Pork, 23
Blueberry Sweet Potato Bread, 33
Bread
    Blueberry Sweet Potato Bread, 33
    Firecracker Cornbread, 108
    German Pioneer Whole Wheat Bread, 25
    Lloyd's Favorite Gingerbread, 44
    Jailhouse Rolls, 133
    Secret of Longevity Sweet Corn Bread, 141
Breakfast Fare
    A Roper's Breakfast, 83
    After the Gig Migas, 14
    Blueberry Sweet Potato Bread, 33
    Coach Gus' Swedish Pancakes, 59
    Coach Penders' Breakfast Tacos, 98
    Migas al Chino, 102
    Out-of-this-World Crab Strata, 84
    Papa Tune's Red Eye Gravy, 127
    Sail Away Breakfast Soufflé, 79
    Sunday Morning Banana Buttermilk
        Pancakes, 19
Broken Spoke's Chicken Fried Steak with
  Cream Gravy, The, 27
Brown Beans by Bullock, 30
Broth, Good and Healthy Chicken, 26
Brownies for Lazy, Decadent People, 68
Bummer Summer Salad, 35
Burritos, Shannon Wheeler's Bachelor, 137

C

Cabrito Frito, Mexican, 144

Cakes
    Italian Cream Cake, 142
    Mayberry Applesauce Cake, 87
    Rosemary and Orange Rum Cake with
        Glorious Glaze, 52
    White Scratch Cake with Texas Pecan Icing, 70
Candy
    As Promised Texas Pralines, 42
Casseroles
    A Treasure of a Tamale Pie, 93
    Grandma's Ham Hallelujah, 94
    King Ranch Chicken, 131
    Make Tracks Chicken, 75
    New Mexico Corn Bake, 101
    No Limits Chicken, 9
    Paella to Flip Over, 107
    Sonora Death Row Casserole, 76
Cheddar Wafers, LBJ Ranch, 72
Cheese Enchiladas, Doctor Time's, 125
Chicken and Fowl
    A Scot's Dutch Witloof by Way of Texas, 91
    Chicken Kale Soup, 28
    Chutney Lime Chicken, 24
    Fat-Freestyle Turkey Chili, 43
    Greenbelt Chicken and Brown Rice Salad, 29
    Gypsy Cowboy Posole, 49
    Hollywood's Chili Beans, 61
    Jane's Drunken Chicken 'n' Dumplins, 37
    Kickin' Chicken Chipotle, 8
    King Ranch Chicken, 131
    Kinkster's Chicken Piccata, The, 53
    Lone Star Pasta Sauce, 7
    Make Tracks Chicken, 75
    Mrs. Barney Miller's Chicken and Mushrooms, 16
    My Ladies' Greek Chicken, 97
    No Limits Chicken, 9
    Paella to Flip Over, 107
    Pollo y Arroz Texas Style, 114
    Roadhouse Pizza, 120
    Ultimate Chicken Spaghetti, The, 36
    Wok 'n' Roll Yardbird Stir Fry, 139
Chicken Fried Steak, The Broken Spoke's, 27
Chicken Fried Steak, Mima's, 134
Chili
    Chuy's Tex-Mex Chili Con Carne, 38

Fat-Freestyle Turkey Chili, 43
Hollywood's Chili Beans, 61
Rave LaFave Veggie Chili, 77
Shadywood Showdown Chili, 66
Texas Chainsaw Chili, 65
Chipotle, Kickin' Chicken, 8
Chocolate Fare
Microwave Chocolate Bread Pudding, 146
Stellar Dessert Meringues, 145
Chutney Lime Chicken, 24
Chuy's Tex-Mex Chili Con Carne, 38
Circle J Pumpkin Risotto, 45
Coach Gus' Swedish Pancakes, 59
Coach Penders' Breakfast Tacos, 98
Congress Avenue Spicy Shrimp, 128
Cookies and Bars
Goodie Bars, 41
Pearl's Molasses Snaps, 115
Slam Dunk Oatmeal Cookies, 39
Stellar Dessert Meringues, 145
Corn
A Master's Creamed Corn, 40
Dill Crusted Salmon with Corn and
  Asparagus Relish, 148
New Mexico Corn Bake, 101
Wheel's Corn Soup, The, 22
Cornbread, Firecracker, 108
Corn Bread, Secret of Longevity Sweet, 141
Corn Soup, The Wheel's, 22
Crab Cakes and Rémoulade, Sweet Potato, 78
Crab Strata, Out-of-this-World, 84

D

Dazed and Confused Lasagna, 138
Desperate for Pecan Pie, 111
Desserts *(see also candy, chocolate fare, cookies and bars, cakes, pies and cobblers, and puddings)*
As Promised Texas Pralines, 42
Beat the Heat Eat Dessert, 116
Blueberry Sweet Potato Bread, 33
Brownies for Lazy, Decadent People, 68
Dewberry Cobbler, 112
Fabulous Noodle Kugel, 31
Lloyd's Favorite Gingerbread, 44
Dewberry Cobbler, 112

Dill Crusted Salmon with Corn and
  Asparagus Relish, 148
Director Héctor Salsa, 55
Doctor Time's Cheese Enchiladas, 125
Dove and Wild Rice, Lonesome, 81
Dove, Honey Butter and Jalapeño, 109
Dreaded Yuppie Sun-dried Tomato Pesto, 74
Dumplins, Jane's Drunken Chicken 'n', 37

E

Earl Campbell's Sausage Jambalaya, 34
Eggs
A Roper's Breakfast, 83
After the Gig Migas, 14
Coach Penders' Breakfast Tacos, 98
Migas al Chino, 102
Out-of-this-World Crab Strata, 84
Enchiladas, Doctor Time's Cheese, 125
Enchiladas, Janet's Spinach, 56
Epicurean Slacker's Delight, 82
Etouffée, Heart of Louisiana, 15

F

Fabulous Noodle Kugel, 31
Fall Creek Basil and Raspberry Shrimp Pasta, 10
Family Style Hot Spaghetti, 129
Fat-Freestyle Turkey Chili, 43
Firecracker Cornbread, 108
Fish and Seafood
Barton Creek Lobster and Vodka Gazpacho, 17
Congress Avenue Spicy Shrimp, 128
Dill Crusted Salmon with Corn and
  Asparagus Relish, 148
Fall Creek Basil and Raspberry Shrimp Pasta, 10
Heart of Louisiana Etouffée, 15
La Zona Rosa's Pasta Gruber, 58
Not-for-the-Capsicum-Impaired Salmon, 12
Out-of-this-World Crab Strata, 84
Paella to Flip Over, 107
Sauced on Tequila Shrimp, 88
Sweet Potato Crab Cakes and Rémoulade, 78
Très Trois Tuna Spaghetti, 126
Fort Smith Apple Pie, 135
Fresh Rodriguez Pico de Gallo, 110

Frostings, Icings, and Glazes
Rosemary and Orange Rum Cake with
  Glorious Glaze, 52
White Scratch Cake with Texas Pecan Icing, 70

G

Gazpacho, Barton Creek Lobster and Vodka, 17
German Pioneer Whole Wheat Bread, 25
German Potato Salad, A Girl's, 57
Gingerbread, Lloyd's Favorite, 44
Go Native Marinade, 54
Go to Hell Prime Rib, 89
Good and Healthy Chicken Broth, 26
Goodie Bars, 41
Grandma's Chilled Peach Pie, 62
Grandma's Ham Hallelujah, 94
Gravy, The Broken Spoke's Chicken Fried Steak
  with Cream, 27
Greek Chicken, My Ladies', 97
Greenbelt Chicken and Brown Rice Salad, 29
Grilled Fare
Arresting Barbecued Pork Loin Chops, 73
Honey Butter and Jalapeño Dove, 109
Kate's Grilled Rack of Lamb, 113
River City Green Bean Rolls, 64
Gypsy Cowboy Posole, 49

H

Ham Hallelujah, Grandma's, 94
Havana Pork Chops, 149
Heart of Louisiana Etouffée, 15
Hollywood's Chili Beans, 61
Honey Butter and Jalapeño Dove, 109
Hungarian Paprika Mushrooms, 69

I

Insalata Pasta e Fagioli, 50
Inside the Eastside Tomato Basil Soup, 48
Italian Cream Cake, 142

J

Jailhouse Rolls, 133

Jamaican Jerked Emu with Mango Chutney, 51
James Michener's Beef Bourguignon, 90
Jane's Drunken Chicken 'n' Dumplins, 37
Janet's Spinach Enchiladas, 56

K

Kale Soup, Chicken, 28
Kate's Grilled Rack of Lamb, 113
Kickin' Chicken Chipotle, 8
King Ranch Chicken, 131
Kinkster's Chicken Piccata, The, 53
Kugel, Fabulous Noodle, 31

L

Lamb
    Kate's Grilled Rack of Lamb, 113

Larry's Almost Thai Chicken Soup, 11
Lasagna, Dazed and Confused, 138
La Zona Rosa's Pasta Gruber, 58
LBJ Ranch Spicy Cheddar Wafers, 72
Leek Soup, Poetic Potato, 60
Lemon Pie, Tequila, 117
Lentil and Spinach Soup, Passionate, 18
Lime Chicken, Chutney, 24
Lime Pie, Vera's, 140
Lloyd's Favorite Gingerbread, 44
Lobster and Vodka Gazpacho, Barton Creek, 17
Lonesome Dove and Wild Rice, 81
Lone Star Pasta Sauce, 7
Lyle Loved It Tart, 106

M

Mac Attack Pasta, 85
Main Course—Beef
    A Cowboy's Favorite Meat Loaf, 6
    A Treasure of a Tamale Pie, 93
    Broken Spoke's Chicken Fried Steak with Cream Gravy, The, 27
    Chuy's Tex-Mex Chili Con Carne, 38
    Go to Hell Prime Rib, 89
    James Michener's Beef Bourguignon, 90
    Mima's Chicken Fried Steak, 134
    Shadywood Showdown Chili, 66
    Texas Chainsaw Chili, 65

Main Course—Chicken and Fowl
    A Scot's Dutch Witloof by Way of Texas, 91
    Chicken Kale Soup, 28
    Chutney Lime Chicken, 24
    Fat-Freestyle Turkey Chili, 43
    Greenbelt Chicken and Brown Rice Salad, 29
    Gypsy Cowboy Posole, 49
    Hollywood's Chili Beans, 61
    Jane's Drunken Chicken 'n' Dumplins, 37
    Kickin' Chicken Chipotle, 8
    King Ranch Chicken, 131
    Kinkster's Chicken Piccata, The, 53
    Lone Star Pasta Sauce, 7
    Make Tracks Chicken, 75
    Mrs. Barney Miller's Chicken and Mushrooms, 16
    My Ladies' Greek Chicken, 97
    No Limits Chicken, 9
    Paella to Flip Over, 107
    Pollo y Arroz Texas Style, 114
    Roadhouse Pizza, 120
    Ultimate Chicken Spaghetti, The, 36
    Wok 'n' Roll Yardbird Stir Fry, 139

Main Course—Fish and Seafood
    Congress Avenue Spicy Shrimp, 128
    Dill Crusted Salmon with Corn and Asparagus Relish, 148
    Fall Creek Basil and Raspberry Shrimp Pasta, 10
    Heart of Louisiana Etouffée, 15
    La Zona Rosa's Pasta Gruber, 58
    Not-for-the-Capsicum-Impaired Salmon, 12
    Out-of-this-World Crab Strata, 84
    Paella to Flip Over, 107
    Sauced on Tequila Shrimp, 88
    Sweet Potato Crab Cakes and Rémoulade, 78
    Très Trois Tuna Spaghetti, 126

Main Course—Goat
    Mexican Cabrito Frito, 144

Main Course—Lamb
    Kate's Grilled Rack of Lamb, 113

Main Course—Pork
    A Scot's Dutch Witloof by Way of Texas, 91
    Arresting Barbecued Pork Loin Chops, 73
    Bevo Tackles Pork, 23
    Earl Campbell's Sausage Jambalaya, 34
    Gypsy Cowboy Posole, 49
    Havana Pork Chops, 149
    Jamaican Jerked Emu with Mango Chutney, 51
    Papa Tune's Red Eye Gravy, 127

Main Course—Veal
    Züricher Geschnizeltes, 96

Main Course—Vegetarian
    Circle J Pumpkin Risotto, 45
    Dazed and Confused Lasagna, 138
    Doctor Time's Cheese Enchiladas, 125
    Janet's Spinach Enchiladas, 56
    Motorolan Moussaka, 130
    Phenomenal Grilled Polenta and Wild Mushroom, 123
    Shannon Wheeler's Bachelor Burritos, 137
    Sinful Texas Tacos, 118
    Sonora Death Row Casserole, 76

Main Course—Wild Game and Fowl
    Bertie's Y.O. Venison, 147
    Honey Butter and Jalapeño Dove, 109
    Lonesome Dove and Wild Rice, 81

Make Tracks Chicken, 75
Mango Chutney, Jamaican Jerked Emu with, 51
Mango Pie, Please, More, 92
Marinade, Go Native, 54
Marinated Portobello Mushrooms with Black Bean Sauce, 46
Mayberry Applesauce Cake, 87
Meat Loaf, A Cowboy's, 6
Meringues, Stellar Dessert, 145
Mexican Cabrito Frito, 144
Microwave Chocolate Bread Pudding, 146
Migas, After the Gig, 14
Migas al Chino, 102
Mima's Chicken Fried Steak, 134
Molasses Snaps, Pearl's, 115
More Mango Pie, Please, 92
Most Famous Hot Sauce In Texas, The, 103
Motorolan Moussaka, 130
Mrs. Barney Miller's Chicken and Mushrooms, 16
Mushrooms
    Hungarian Paprika Mushrooms, 69
    Marinated Portobello Mushrooms with Black Bean Sauce, 46
    Mrs. Barney Miller's Chicken and Mushrooms, 16
    Phenomenal Grilled Polenta and Wild Mushroom Napoleon, 123

My Father's Tuna Spread, 143
My Ladies' Greek Chicken, 97
My Mom's Vinegar Pie, 104

N

New Mexico Corn Bake, 101
No Limits Chicken, 9
Noodle Kugel, Fabulous, 31
Not-for-the-Capsicum-Impaired Salmon, 12

O

Orange Rum Cake with Glorious Glaze, Rosemary and, 52
Orzo, A Woman on the Verge of Herbed, 95
Out-of-this-World Crab Strata, 84

P

Paella to Flip Over, 107
Pancakes
    Coach Gus' Swedish Pancakes, 59
    Sunday Morning Banana Buttermilk Pancakes, 19
Papa Tune's Red Eye Gravy, 127
Passionate Lentil and Spinach Soup, 18
Pasta
    A Woman on the Verge of Herbed Orzo, 95
    Dazed and Confused Lasagna, 138
    Dreaded Yuppie Sun-dried Tomato Pesto, 74
    Fall Creek Basil and Raspberry Shrimp Pasta, 10
    Family Style Hot Spaghetti, 129
    Insalata Pasta e Fagioli, 50
    Kinkster's Chicken Piccata, The, 53
    La Zona Rosa's Pasta Gruber, 58
    Lone Star Pasta Sauce, 7
    Mac Attack Pasta, 85
    Mrs. Barney Miller's Chicken and Mushrooms, 16
    Pasta Talbot, 121
    Roasted Red Bell Pepper Pesto, 71
    Ruby's El Paso 1949 Pasta, 20
    Speedy Pasta e Fagioli, 119
    Très Trois Tuna Spaghetti, 126
    Twice-Naked Pesto, 99
    Ultimate Chicken Spaghetti, The, 36
Pattypan Squash with a Twist, 80

Peaches
    Award Winning Texas Sweet Peach Cobbler, 122
    Grandma's Chilled Peach Pie, 62
Pearl's Molasses Snaps, 115
Pecans
    As Promised Texas Pralines, 42
    Desperate for Pecan Pie, 111
    Statehouse Pecan Pie, 32
    White Scratch Cake with Texas Pecan Icing, 70
Pesto
    Dreaded Yuppie Sun-dried Tomato Pesto, 74
    Roasted Red Bell Pepper Pesto, 71
    Twice-Naked Pesto, 99
Phenomenal Grilled Polenta and Wild Mushroom Napoleon, 123
Pies and Cobblers
    Award Winning Texas Sweet Peach Cobbler, 122
    Desperate for Pecan Pie, 111
    Dewberry Cobbler, 112
    Fort Smith Apple Pie, 135
    Grandma's Chilled Peach Pie, 62
    Lyle Loved It Tart, 106
    More Mango Pie, Please, 92
    My Mom's Vinegar Pie, 104
    Statehouse Pecan Pie, 32
    Tequila Lemon Pie, 117
    Vera's Lime Pie, 140
    Veronique's Apple Pie, 86
    Vinegar Pie, My Mom's, 104
Pico de Gallo, Fresh Rodriguez, 110
Pizza, Roadhouse, 120
Poetic Potato Leek Soup, 60
Polenta and Wild Mushroom Napoleon, Phenomenal Grilled, 123
Pollo y Arroz Texas Style, 114
Pork
    A Scot's Dutch Witloof by Way of Texas, 91
    Arresting Barbecued Pork Loin Chops, 73
    Bevo Tackles Pork, 23
    Earl Campbell's Sausage Jambalaya, 34
    Gypsy Cowboy Posole, 49
    Havana Pork Chops, 149
    Jamaican Jerked Emu with Mango Chutney, 51
    Papa Tune's Red Eye Gravy, 127
Posole, Gypsy Cowboy, 49

Potatoes
    A Girl's German Potato Salad, 57
    A Scot's Dutch Witloof by Way of Texas, 91
    Barn Dance Potluck Potato Salad, 100
    Grandma's Ham Hallelujah, 94
    No Limits Chicken, 9
    Poetic Potato Leek Soup, 60
    Rosemary Garlic Roasted Potatoes, 105
    Zilker Park Picnic for 50, 13
Pralines, As Promised Texas, 42
Prime Rib, Go to Hell, 89
Puddings
    Microwave Chocolate Bread Pudding, 146
    Shade Tree Banana Pudding, 47
Pumpkin Risotto, Circle J, 45

R

Rave LaFave Veggie Chili, 77
Red Bell Pepper Pesto, Roasted, 71
Relish, Dill Crusted Salmon with Corn and Asparagus, 148
Rice
    Circle J Pumpkin Risotto, 45
    Earl Campbell's Sausage Jambalaya, 34
    Greenbelt Chicken and Brown Rice Salad, 29
    Lonesome Dove and Wild Rice, 81
    Paella to Flip Over, 107
    Pollo y Arroz Texas Style, 114
    River City Green Bean Rolls, 64
River City Green Bean Rolls, 64
Roadhouse Pizza, 120
Roasted Red Bell Pepper Pesto, 71
Rolls, Jailhouse, 133
Rosemary and Orange Rum Cake with Glorious Glaze, 52
Rosemary Garlic Roasted Potatoes, 105
Ruby's El Paso 1949 Pasta, 20

S

Sail Away Breakfast Soufflé, 79
Salads
    A Girl's German Potato Salad, 57
    Barn Dance Potluck Potato Salad, 100
    Bummer Summer Salad, 35

Greenbelt Chicken and Brown Rice Salad, 29
Insalata Pasta e Fagioli, 50
Zilker Park Picnic for 50, 13
Salmon
    Dill Crusted Salmon with Corn and Asparagus Relish, 148
    Not-for-the-Capsicum-Impaired Salmon, 12
Salsa
    Director Héctor Salsa, 55
    Fresh Rodriguez Pico de Gallo, 110
    The Most Famous Hot Sauce In Texas, 103
Sauce, Traditional Ancho, 63
Sauced on Tequila Shrimp, 88
Sausage
    A Roper's Breakfast, 83
    Earl Campbell's Sausage Jambalaya, 34
    Lone Star Pasta Sauce, 7
Secret of Longevity Sweet Corn Bread, 141
Shade Tree Banana Pudding, 47
Shadywood Showdown Chili, 66
Shannon Wheeler's Bachelor Burritos, 137
Shrimp
    Congress Avenue Spicy Shrimp, 128
    Fall Creek Basil and Raspberry Shrimp Pasta, 10
    Heart of Louisiana Etoufée, 15
    Sauced on Tequila Shrimp, 88
Sinful Texas Tacos, 118
Slackers
    Epicurean Slackers Delight, 82
Slam Dunk Oatmeal Cookies, 39
Sonora Death Row Casserole, 76
Soufflé, Sail Away Breakfast, 79
Soup *(also see chili)*
    Barton Creek Lobster and Vodka Gazpacho, 17
    Chicken Kale Soup, 28
    Gypsy Cowboy Posole, 49
    Inside the Eastside Tomato Basil Soup, 48
    Jane's Drunken Chicken 'n' Dumplins, 37
    Larry's Almost Thai Chicken Soup, 11
    Poetic Potato Leek Soup, 60
    Passionate Lentil and Spinach Soup, 18
    The Wheel's Corn Soup, 22
Spaghetti, Family Style Hot, 129
Spaghetti, The Ultimate Chicken, 36
Speedy Pasta e Fagioli, 119
Spicy Shrimp, Congress Avenue, 128

Spinach Enchiladas, Janet's, 56
Squash with a Twist, Pattypan, 80
Statehouse Pecan Pie, 32
Stellar Dessert Meringues, 145
Sunday Morning Banana Buttermilk Pancakes, 19
Swedish Pancakes, Coach Gus', 59
Sweet Potato Bread, Blueberry, 33
Sweet Potato Crab Cakes and Rémoulade, 78

T

Tacos, Coach Penders' Breakfast, 98
Tacos, Sinful Texas, 118
Tamale Pie, A Treasure of a, 93
Tequila Lemon Pie, 117
Texas Chainsaw Chili, 65
Thai Chicken Soup, Larry's Almost, 11
Tomato Basil Soup, Inside the Eastside, 48
Tomato Pesto, Dreaded Yuppie Sun-dried, 74
Traditional Ancho Sauce, 63
Très Trois Tuna Spaghetti, 126
Tuna Spread, My Father's, 143
Twice-Naked Pesto, 99

U

Ultimate Chicken Spaghetti, The, 36

V

Veal
    Züricher Geschnitzeltes, 96
Vegetarian Fare or Vegetables *(see also beans, corn, mushrooms, potatoes, and zucchini)*
    Circle J Pumpkin Risotto, 45
    Dazed and Confused Lasagna, 138
    Doctor Time's Cheese Enchiladas, 125
    Dreaded Yuppie Sun-dried Tomato Pesto, 74
    Janet's Spinach Enchiladas, 56
    Mac Attack, 85
    Motorolan Moussaka, 130
    Pasta Talbot, 121
    Pattypan Squash with a Twist, 80
    Phenomenal Grilled Polenta and Wild Mushroom Napoleon, 123
    Rave LaFave Veggie Chili, 77

River City Green Bean Rolls, 64
Roasted Red Bell Pepper Pesto, 71
Ruby's El Paso 1949 Pasta, 20
Shannon Wheeler's Bachelor Burritos, 137
Sinful Texas Tacos, 118
Sonora Death Row Casserole, 76
Speedy Pasta e Fagioli, 119
Twice-Naked Pesto, 99
Venison, Bertie's Y.O., 147
Vera's Lime Pie, 140
Veronique's Apple Pie, 86
Vinegar Pie, My Mom's, 104

W

Wheel's Corn Soup, The, 22
White Scratch Cake with Texas Pecan Icing, 70
Whole Wheat Bread, German Pioneer, 25
Wild Game and Fowl
    Bertie's Y.O. Venison, 147
    Honey Butter and Jalapeño Dove, 109
    Lonesome Dove and Wild Rice, 81
Witloof by Way of Texas, A Scot's Dutch, 91
Wok 'n' Roll Yardbird Stir Fry, 139

Z

Zilker Park Picnic for 50, 13
Zucchini
    Anhydrous Zucchini, 136
    Züricher Geschnitzeltes, 96

Thank You, Thank You, Thank You

First, thanks to each and every recipe contributor who took time from busy and demanding schedules to send a recipe, convey an anecdote, and to suggest other contributors.

A bigger-than-the-state-of-Texas thanks to our new friends at the Austin Parks Foundation. Paula Fracasso is the best executive director, ever, and we are thankful for her input, guidance, and contacts. Thanks to Beverly Griffith, past president, for making that first phone call and suggesting the idea. Thanks to Robin Redford for following up on details. Thanks to Nancy Bowman for her ability to get recipes from very busy and very famous people. Thanks to John Howard, Shirley Deininger, and Carlton Schwab for their creative ideas, feedback, and enthusiasm.

Special Thanks to *Austin City Limits*, and most especially to Susan Caldwell Halley and Daniel Zmud for sharing research and connections. Also, Julia Null Smith at the Texas Office of Music, Film, Television and Multimedia. Jann Baskett and Lisa Lawrence at *Texas Monthly*. Ann Hinshaw at the Texas Film Commission. Thanks all— for your time, generosity, ideas, and information.

Thanks to Joan Donnelly for your creativity, patience, endurance, and always giving us options. Will Caldwell, for being an artist with a social conscience. Our recipe reader, food guru and friend, Rory Farrow. When's dinner, Rory? Thanks to Amy Stahl and Rond Reid for catching the commas, hyphens, honers, clinkers, and goots. To our own personal tour guide, Renee Villenueve. Thanks, Andy Phillips, for making it as easy as possible. Bill McMahan, project coordinator and director of marketing. Ra Ra Ra to our cheerleader, Ray Mondo. To Helen Howard for watching out for things on the national scene. As always, Robert J. Willert, for celebrity information and expertise. Julie Driver for sharing your design expertise with us. Thanks to Spa and Craig at Magic Mountain Music for making our living rooms rock and for knowing what goes on outside of lala land. Very special thanks to Margo Winter, Karen Word, and Micki Balderas at the Driskill for a room with a view. And to the memory of Ken Slike: May your musical talents live on with Emily and Sam.

To our testing kitchen and their guinea pig families and friends: Millie Reid, Bonnie Scudder, Ronda Cannon, John Kampschror, Sofia Jaramillo, Ruby Bleu, and Mary and George Lane.

And to the people in the background that made it happen: managers, agents, publicists, wives, husbands, friends, and moms. You know who you are. Thanks for persevering: Aikman Enterprises and Charlyne, Steve Akers, Patricia Alholm, Arista Texas and Carrie Prince, *Austin Chronicle*, Austin Federation of Musicians Local 43 and Kim Beleu and CJ, Andi Ball, Ballet Austin and Lambros Lambrou and Andi Cadena, Helen Ballew, Craig Barker, Barton Creek Resort and Ken Manceaux, Baruch Consolo Management, Bat Conservation International and Marla Crump, Diane Begala, Bismeaux Productions

Very special thanks from the Austin Parks Foundation to:

Authors

Nancy Reid of Boise, Idaho, and Sheila Liermann of Ketchum, Idaho, began compiling and publishing celebrity cookbooks in 1992 and have been in a constant state of panic since. Their first cookbook, the *Sun Valley Celebrity & Local Heroes Cookbook*, was published as a benefit for the Advocates for Survivors of Domestic Violence. Royalties from the sale of the *Utah Celebrity & Local Heroes Cookbook* benefit the Park City Performing Arts Center. *Famous Friends of the Wolf Cookbook* was released by Adams Media Corporation in October, 1996. A royalty from the sale of each *Famous Friend's* cookbook is paid to the Wolf Education & Research Center. Royalties from the sale of the *Austin & Hill Country Celebrity Cookbook* benefit the Austin Parks Foundation.

(Thanks continued)
and Asleep at the Wheel and Ray Benson and Susan Griswold, Julie Blinn, Book People and Jerry Cunningham, Andrea Broyles, Al Bunetta Management, George Burton, Office of George Bush Jr. and Linda Poepsel, CBS News and Sakura Komiyama and Amy Bennett, Earl Campbell Food Products and Jennifer, Continental Club, Mike Crowley Management, John Davies, Shantel Davis, Conrad Deisler, Detour Filmproduction and Brian, dos records, The Driskill and Michael Burke, Marc Eberstein, Edge Management and Kathleen Keen, Ray E. Edmundson, Encino Press, Far Flung Adventures, Debbie Farquhar-Garner, Charlene E. Fern, Nancy Fly and Associates, *Fort Worth Star-Telegram* and Liz Faulk, Gordon Fowler, Pam Francis, Cindy at Fredericksburg Herb Farm, Galán Productions and Leah Marino, Earnie Gammaga and Gambini Global, Janet Gilmore, Girl Games, Inc. and Eli Grill, Wendy Goldstein, Dan Goodman, Greater Tuna Corporation and Carla McQueen, Janet Griffin, Hatchett Talent, Cleve Hattersley, Pat Hingle, Wendy Hopkins, Hot Sauce Festival and Elizabeth Dirkso, Huston-Tillotson College and Sandy Wilder, International Creative Management, JTP Films and Kim Ryusaki, Shirley James, Terry Jonas, Kathleen Keen and Edge Management, Laguna Entertainment, Lake Austin Spa Resort and Janis Simms, Barbara Logan and Meanwhile Management, Los Hooligans Production, Amy Lowrey, Lovell Communications and Mary Weeks, Ma N Pa Management, Mango, Gary Marburger, Veronique Matthews, McGuckin Entertainment Group and Jill McGuckin, Davis McLarty, Susan Morehead, Motorola and Julie Grissom, Music Capital Management, Page Nordstrom, Ruth S. Nunn, PMA and Shep Goldberg, Paint Rock Productions and Sheila Gallien, Pet Sharks, Joe Priesnitz, Proper Marketing Associates and Barbara J. Scheve, Press Corps Inc. and Kate Wicker, QBQ Entertainment and Lori Angelo, Frank Racine, Edith Royal, Rudolf R. Scheffrahn, Gus Schreiner, Siegel and Feldstein, Specialty Films and Linda Craigen, Rita Stamel, Harriet Sternberg Management and Paula Bonhomme, Stress Management and Jeff Tartakov, Kathy Stitina, Tom Sutton, Janet Syms, Tried and True Music and Gwen Robison, University of Texas and Robert Tindol and Rita Stramel, University of Texas Athetic Department and Nancy Perryman, University of Texas McDonald Observatory, Susan Walker, James White, Paula White, Wildfire Productions, William Morris Agency, Randy Willis, Madrile Wilson, Cindy Youngblood, Marcia Zwilling

Austin & Hill Country Celebrity Cookbook Order Form

Ordered by:

Name: _____

Address: _____

City: _____ State: _____

Zip Code: _____ Telephone: (_____)_____

Please send ____ book(s) at $20 each for a total of $_____
Plus Sales Tax:
  Austin residents send sales tax of $1.65 per book
  Other Texas residents send sales tax of $1.45 per book $_____

Plus Shipping & Handling of $3.00 per book $_____

TOTAL ENCLOSED: $_____

Please make checks payable to the Austin Parks Foundation.
Please do not send cash. Sorry, no C.O.D.s.

Ship to: (if other than the above address)

Name: _____

Address: _____

City: _____ State: _____

Zip Code: _____ Telephone: (_____)_____

All royalties benefit the Austin Parks Foundation.

Send to: Austin Parks Foundation, 2112 Rio Grande, Austin, Texas 78705
          Phone: 512-477-1566